Praise for *Survivor*

"*Survivor*'s sociological, pseudo-Machiavellian aspect makes it the
antithesis of traditional quiz shows . . . . On *Survivor*, it's as much who you
know, and what they think of you . . . . The psychological rigors of two score days
in the rain forest—and the potential humiliation of being booted by fifteen
comrades on national television—are as worrisome as the jungle fauna."
—*Time*

"Cinéma vérité with an Orwellian aura is finding a home on
American television . . . . *Survivor* breaks the mold of comedies, dramas,
and news programs . . . . This is Peeping Tom to the max."
—*The New York Times*

"What's being tested here isn't whether any of these people can
survive on an uninhabited island, but whether they can survive one
another, and how they negotiate the conflict between their selfish,
competitive instincts and their need to preserve group strength."
—*Nancy Franklin in the New Yorker*

"*Survivor*, the well-produced, irresistible, inessential, and insanely
successful hybrid of fantasy and reality, has changed television."
—*Inside TV*

"*Survivor* is quickly working its way into American pop culture."
—*USA Today*

"The unofficial water-cooler show."
—*Minneapolis Star Tribune*

"Not only is *Survivor* the biggest-ever launch of a summer series,
but it beats all the time-slot competition combined."
—*Inside.com*

"*Survivor* now ranks as the most watched summer
primetime series in modern televison history."
—*Hollywood Reporter*

"Fascinating entertainment, the kind that people will be talking about."
—*New York Post*

"The hottest show in America."
—*TV Guide*

SURVIVOR II
The Field Guide

The Official Companion to
the CBS Television Show

MARK BURNETT

TV Books
NEW YORK

Scott Duncan still photographs © 2001 Survivor
Productions, LLC.

Photographs on pages 35, 39, 52, and 62 courtesy
of Corbis.

Map on page 43 courtesy of Eyewire.

Library of Congress Cataloging-in-Publication Data
available on request.

TV Books, LLC
1619 Broadway
New York, NY 10019
www.tvbooks.com

Interior design by Timothy J. Shaner
Pull-out map by Joe Gannon
Manufactured in the United States of America

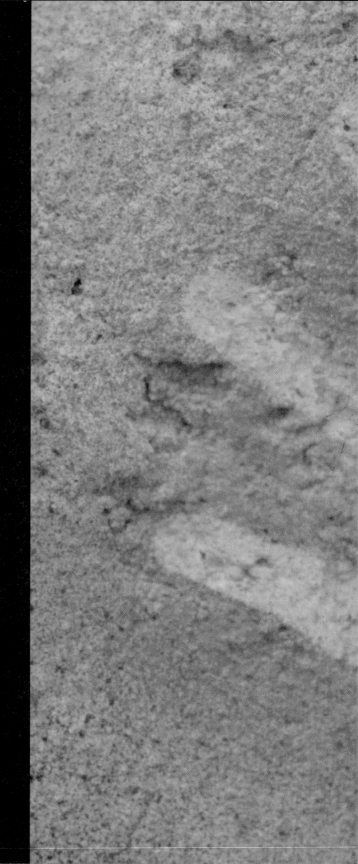

*Dedicated to
those who take risks.*

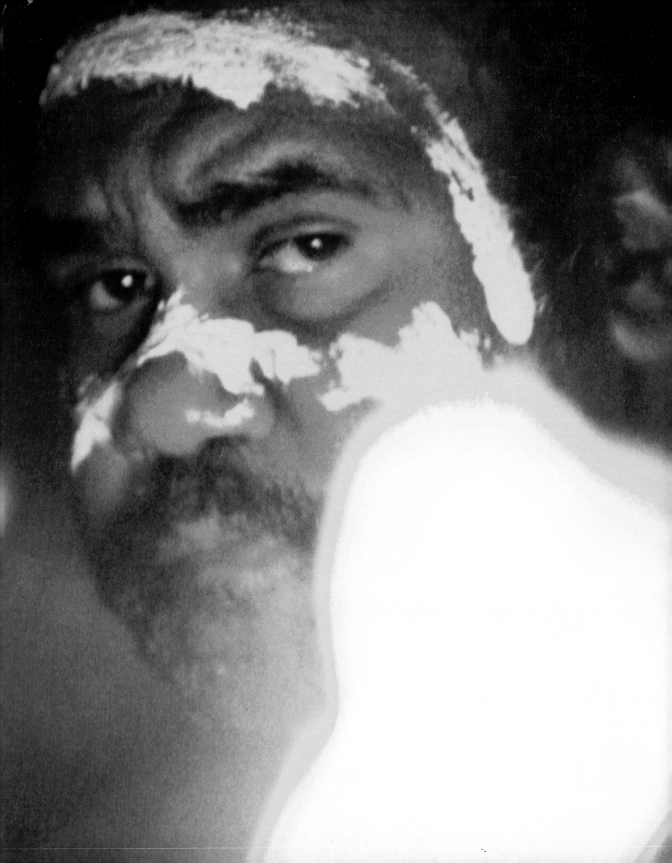

Contents

Prologue

Mark Burnett

On January 28, 2001, immediately after Super Bowl XXXV, American television viewers will be transported to the Australian outback for the second edition of *Survivor*. The little dramality show that took the country by storm will return. Sixteen new contestants will endeavor to outwit, outplay, and outlast each other for the million-dollar first prize. They will eat strange food and endure perilous living conditions. They will be challenged for rewards and immunity. They will love and steal and laugh and lie under a broiling Australian sun. And by the show's finale, fourteen episodes later, these men and women and their survival strategies will be famous—or, in some cases, infamous.

Before the games begin, however, it might be fruitful to step back and take a look at every aspect of the *Survivor* game: players, strategies, conditions, challenges. This book offers readers a unique portal into the *Survivor* experience, sharing insights about the players, the playing field, and the game that will be found nowhere else. Indeed, readers will know more about Australia and its perils than the contestants themselves do before filming begins.

So much will have happened between the final Tribal Council of *Survivor: Borneo* and the moment Jeff Probst divides the group of sixteen contestants for *Survivor: The Australian Outback* into two tribes and abandons them in the outback. The summer of 2000 saw the show vault into America's consciousness in a huge way. Suddenly, people began wondering if they had what it took to play the *Survivor* game, and how they would play it if they did. Some even realized that they were already playing the game, although in their daily lives instead of on a remote island. That collective experience was the underlying humanity of the show, and one of the most significant reasons a record audience tuned in to watch the August 23 finale.

Survivor, then, is not a singular experience, conducted on a deserted tropical island or in the Australian outback, but a collective struggle between sixteen adventurous men and women. *Survivor* as a TV show is Pulau Tiga and Australia and a host of other exotic locations not yet determined. But *Survivor* is also your home, your office, your school—wherever men and women struggle to coexist.

Let's begin the journey to *Survivor: The Australian Outback* with a behind-the-scenes look at that final Tribal Council on Pulau Tiga. The countdown to Australia, and the book you're reading now, began then.

Chapter One

Survivor: Borneo

Last Days

April 20, 2000, sunrise. Pulau Tiga. Susan Hawk paces the beach, trying to organize her thoughts. *Survivor's* final Tribal Council will be held in a little over twelve hours and she wants to make a definitive statement about her time on the island. "I don't know what I'm going to say, but I want to make a speech tonight," she says. "I don't know whether I'm going to vote for Richard or Kelly, because I don't like either of them. There's just a lot of things I need to get off my chest and I plan to spend the whole day trying to figure out what that is and who I'm voting for."

Sue made it to *Survivor's* final four but was expelled the night before last during an Immunity Challenge known as "Fallen Comrades." The island game was basically a quiz show that asked castaways to recall trivia about castaways previously voted off. Host Jeff Probst asked questions such as "Whose shirt is this?" as he passed around one of Jenna's tattered island belongings. It all came down to the final question which would award Sue or Kelly immunity. As the other two members of the final four, Richard and Rudy, looked on, Probst asked the two women to remember one final detail: "What was Sonja's," he asked, referring to the first castaway voted off, thirty-seven long days and nights of island living earlier, "last name?"

Kelly knew the answer was "Christopher." Sue did not. Having won her fourth consecutive Immunity Challenge, Kelly was in no danger of being voted off when it came time to narrow the castaways to a final three. It was Kelly who cast the vote to send Sue off the island. The two women had once sworn to stick together through thick and thin, until *Survivor's* final two. Their partnership had fractured as the days to the final Tribal Council grew near, with Kelly making secret pacts with

OPPOSITE: Dirk

RIGHT: Richard

It's not by doing the things we like, but by liking the things we do that we can discover life's blessings.

—Goethe

Kelly

Richard that destroyed whatever trust Sue had in her young friend. They'd argued bitterly on the white sands of Tagi Beach, swearing and crying until there was no doubt *Survivor* had reduced what was left of their relationship to a struggle for the million-dollar first prize. It wasn't necessarily a surprise when Kelly voted Sue off the island, but it was still an act of betrayal in Sue's eyes. The thirty-eight-year-old Wisconsin truck driver had stated several times during her six weeks on Pulau Tiga that she valued loyalty over almost any other quality. She wanted revenge.

On the other hand, Rich had been sneaky and backstabbing since their first day on the island. For the sake of his status in the game, Rich lied. He manipulated in the most Machiavellian fashion. He played Sue and Kelly against each other to build greater loyalty to himself. The fact that he strolled around naked, his immense girth not quite concealing his private parts, was a non-issue for Sue. Nudity didn't bother her. The fact that Rich played her for a fool, however, was hurtful. One such instance came just after Probst extinguished Sue's torch and ended her time as a castaway by intoning "The tribe has spoken." Richard called out "Love ya, Sue!" as she walked alone into the night. His tone was meant to be sincere and playful, but it sounded mocking. Despite a sometimes cold exterior, Sue is also remarkably warm and totally committed to her family. Though Sue played the part of the dumb redneck, she's in fact articulate and well-read. She doesn't like anyone playing her for a fool.

Kelly won Immunity again the day after Sue was ousted, outlasting Richard and Rudy in "Hands on a Hard Idol." The Challenge basically amounted to the physical embodiment of the Survivor maxim to "Outlast," with the three standing on stumps in the blazing sun, slathered in gray mud that tightened and cracked as the temperature rose, keeping one hand on the Immunity idol at all times. The last one with their hand on the idol won.

Pulau Tiga was especially hot that day, with the temperature well over 100°F (38° Celsius) before 10:00 A.M. The sky was cloudless. A storm the previous night had drenched the earth and left behind soaking humidity to go with the heat. As the three remaining Survivors stood in a circle atop their stumps, fidgeting and shifting their weight from one foot to another but always keeping one hand on the Immunity Idol, the production crew congregated out of camera range. They nibbled orange slices, read books, napped, or hovered under the large white tent, sipping ice-cold bottled water. Probst made occasional forays on-camera to banter with the castaways, interviewing them and interjecting tension and controversy into the tedium.

Rudy wasn't talking much, nor was Kelly, but Rich was happy to share his thoughts about strategy. His tone was coy, as if he knew something no one else was aware of. Richard could be a bit of a blowhard, but when it came to island strategy, anything he had to say was insightful. Eighteen days before, when the island still had half its original residents, that master schemer had stood off-camera and told Probst exactly which individuals would be voted off all the way to the show's end—and in the proper order. He had not been wrong once. Compared with Rich's master strategizing, the rest of the contestants were passive participants.

Probst eventually brought cold glasses of water and slices of orange to the thirsty, starving castaways. He placed them just out of reach. If they wanted to eat or drink, hands would need to be removed from the hard idol.

Richard broke. It was surprising, though, that he hadn't done it earlier. He was a long shot to win the Immunity Challenge, easily given to boredom and disliking physical discomfort. Also, Kelly and Rudy were tenacious and stubborn, unlikely to quit. But most important, Rich knew he wouldn't be voted off. If Rudy won the Immunity Challenge he would oust Kelly because he'd sworn loyalty to Rich. If Kelly won, she would oust Rudy because the ex–Navy SEAL was the most popular remaining castaway. With the ultimate winner being chosen by a jury of former castaways, Kelly would lose a popularity contest with Rudy. But winning a popularity contest with Richard? No problem. He was admired for his cunning, but otherwise universally loathed. Richard liked to talk about his close circle of friends cheering him on back home in Rhode Island, but he had no friends on Pulau Tiga. Richard was safe.

Rudy

Two hours later, Rudy took his hand off the idol. But where Richard had stepped from his stump with an air of grandeur, Rudy made a slight mistake. While shifting positions, he removed his hand for an instant. No one in the crew saw the slip, and Rudy was unaware that he'd done it. After hours in the sun, his body encased in a hard mud shell, his mind was on autopilot. But Kelly saw. She cried out to Probst and anyone else who would pay attention, "He took his hand off!" Rudy looked at the sand and shook his head in disgust. He'd said all along that he could win *Survivor* if he didn't do "something dumb." Well, he had. That night, just as he knew she would, Kelly voted Rudy off. The Kern River whitewater guide walked across the Tribal Council set into the voting booth to do it, but she might as well have pointed a finger at Rudy and told him to go home. In the confessional, that post-ousting vent into a small camera just off the Tribal Council set, Rudy didn't offer the long rants other castaways had indulged in. "I screwed up," was all he said.

That night Rudy joined Sue and the other five castaways comprising *Survivor's* jury—Gervase, Greg, Colleen, Jenna, Sean—in a compound specially prepared for them. Throughout the filming, exiled castaways had been taking the three-hour boat ride on the *Sea Quest VII*, followed by a bus ride through the small villages of Borneo, to the Magellan Sutera hotel in Kota Kinabalu, after they were voted off. They'd come back every three days to watch subsequent Tribal Councils, spending the night in a small tent city on the beach before traveling back to stay at the Magellan Sutera until the next Tribal Council. However, there was a Tribal Council each of the last three nights of *Survivor*. The jury remained on the island. Their tent city was on the same side of Pulau Tiga as the production crew's compound, but on the opposite side of the island from where they'd spent their time as contestants, at least a mile of dense jungle distant. Though the production crew was just a quarter mile down the beach, the jury was kept separate for fear their votes would be influenced.

This is where Sue stands on the morning of Day Thirty-Nine. The other six jurors are nearby. Rudy does his morning workout of pushups and jumping jacks. Gervase, Greg, Colleen, and Jenna walk along the surf line, trying to decide whether to clean up with a swim. Sean sips coffee as he contemplates the night to come. No one, however, approaches Sue. Her crossed arms and tight smile say in clear body language that she wants to be alone. Her pacing is deliberate, punctuated by sweeping arm gestures. "Whatever I say tonight," she says to a nearby crew member, "I want people to remember it. I'm a hunter. I've got both guns loaded. All the way. I'm going to fire 'em full blast."

Sue

Final Tribal Council

Except for the Tribal Council set, the island goes dark as the production compound's generators are shut down. This is a regular part of Tribal Council procedure, ensuring not just the proper night environment for filming, but quiet—at full thrum, the generators are as loud as chain saws.

For each of the other fourteen Tribal Councils, the quieting of the generators was the signal for the production crew to tramp into the jungle to the Tribal Council set. Like Romans watching gladiator battles, the writers and art directors and producers and production assistants gathered just offstage to await the castaways' arrival. Seeing who would get voted off next was big theater, and a welcome payoff for the hard days and nights filming around the clock. Applying mosquito repellent in hot weather or donning raincoats during storms, the hundred-person crew gathered rapt and silent for the great entertainment they reveled in filming. Often they would be joined by thirty or so Malaysians who had been brought to the island to assist with production.

Tonight is different. *Survivor's* popularity depends upon secrecy. Public knowledge of the winner's name will rob the show, with all its months of preparation and weeks of filming, of its natual suspense. From Hollywood, executives at CBS have been making frantic calls to Pulau Tiga's single phone all day, seeking reassurance that secrecy is being maintained—that every single detail of the finale is under lock and key. The production crew members have all signed confidentiality agreements stating that they will not reveal details of *Survivor*, with a multi-million dollar penalty for indiscretion. Despite this, many of the Americans understand that they will be excluded from the set in order to keep those "who know" to an absolute minimum. The Malaysians, however, may become offended, so to avoid this, the decision is made to close the set. The audience for the final Tribal Council will be limited to mandatory personnel only—producers, camera and sound crews, lighting, and art department. The remainder of the crew are asked to remain in the production compound during filming. A massive feast is being planned for the wrap party, with barbecued lamb and chicken, an open bar, and a live band setting up on a stage built just for the occasion.

A security team has patrolled the island throughout filming, protecting crew and castaways from Malaysian smugglers (the waters off nearby Snake Island are a favorite rendezvous site for their speedboats) and snooping tabloid journalists. A journalist from *Outside* magazine will later claim he hired a boat in KK and breached Pulau Tiga security by sneaking ashore. The possibility of such an action has kept security on their toes. Tonight, with the *Survivor* franchise threatened by even the slightest leak, these men (Malaysian commandos in the employ of an elite Hong Kong firm specializing in protecting heads of state and celebrities) form a tight perimeter around the Tribal Council set. They stand in the jungle darkness, facing outward, dressed in camouflage. Every man carries an automatic weapon.

On the set, the skeleton crew await the castaways. Probst paces near his mark, talking to himself. He works without a script, preferring to spend the hours before Tribal Council jotting notes on three-by-five-inch cards about each castaway, often role-playing to imagine how each castaway will react to certain questions. In the final moments before filming, he and I confer. We speak in shorthand, and I offer specific words or phrases that I'd like Jeff to say on-camera or to a specific castaway. During the filming itself, I always come to the voting booth to give Jeff the order to read votes. For the most part, however, Probst improvises. The only scripted words he has used are "The tribe has spoken," "Fire represents life," and "Time for you to go." Probst likes to joke that he'll come back on the set after counting the votes one day and say "Is that your final answer?" instead of "The tribe has spoken."

Meanwhile, a few hundred yards offstage in the jungle, a sound engineer is fitting Rich and Kelly with lavaliere microphones. They've spent all day burning the detritus of Tagi Beach—things like Sean's infamous Super Pole 2000 and the communal eating utensils that stood as markers of the time on Pulau Tiga. Rich does not traditionally carry his belongings to Tribal Council with him, but since this will be the finale, he has a small pack over his shoulder. Inside are his keepsakes of the island, including a small needlepoint framed by driftwood that Kelly made for

Sean and Super Pole 2000

Rudy that reads "Rowdy Rudy's Diner." Rudy had been the Tagi (later Rattana) tribe's cook, and often passed spare time sitting before the fire, staring out to sea or quietly observing his fellow castaways. The needlepoint was an acknowledgment that the eating area was Rudy's domain.

After a sound check, and after word comes by walkie-talkie from the Tribal Council set that everyone and everything is in position, a production assistant checks both Rich and Kelly's torches. One of those torches will be extinguished by the final vote.

And then they walk to the set, guided by the light of their torches.

Approaching the set that final time, Rich and Kelly feel the eyes of the small crowd of onlookers.

The night would have been warm and comfortable under any other circumstances, enhanced by a gentle breeze blowing in as the tide went out. But the tension is awful. One of the two will go home a millionaire (second place is $100,000—not exactly small change), and will know incredible happiness in less than an hour. Now, though, it is awful to watch them. They are nervous and tense and painfully aware that every instant of what is happening is being recorded for national television. Their success or failure will be a matter of public record.

Gretchen

They bang the Tribal Council gong as they enter. Probst awaits at the far side of the stage. Rich and Kelly take seats by the fire. The jury is ushered in. All realize that this is their last on-camera moment for *Survivor*. Though they won't win the million, any last thoughts or vendettas must be expressed in this forum.

After his usual introductory remarks, Probst gets down to business. He reminds everyone why they've come halfway around the world. "If the contest were for the sweetest contestant, Gretchen or Sonja might be getting the final vote. If it were for most athletic, Gervase or Joel might be the victor . . . but this is about survival."

Kelly looks down, trying to make eye contact with no one. Rich, on the other hand, gazes across the fire at the jury as if to remind them that survival's been his aim all along. "Forget how I've acted, forget what I've said. Remember that I've played the game well, though, and admire me for it."

When Probst gives the two finalists a chance to offer opening remarks a moment later, that's exactly what Richard says. He thinks the jury should vote according to who played the game well, regardless of their personality tics.

Kelly says almost exactly the opposite, reminding people that she treated them well and was their friend. Playing the game in a Machiavellian way isn't what it's about.

Probst takes a minute to let both sets of comments sink in. Those standing offstage are absorbed in the process, as the castaways' words carry easily through the still jungle night. Even the normal cacophony of night bugs is quiet, save a large flying bug caught in one of the lights. His wings make a

Jenna

loud clickety-clack sound until he finally lets go of his fascination.

Probst, noting again that this is not a normal Tribal Council, tells the jury that they'll be allowed one question or statement to the castaways. Gervase and Jenna go first, asking polite questions that Kelly and Rich field easily. Sean goes next, doing a little shtick about Fat Naked Fag (Richard's sitcom idea) and recalling good times on the island.

From the way the first three talk, it seems Gervase and Jenna favor Kelly, while Sean favors Rich.

Colleen gets up next. She's always been considered the mild-mannered castaway, but her competitive fire has been stoked. Though she asks each castaway a simple question about traits that allowed them to get so far, her follow-up response to Richard's answer is the first contrary note of the evening. Rich claims that his best trait was observation of his fellow castaways (Kelly's were faith and likability). Colleen looks almost irate when Rich answers, as if he's either lying to her or expecting her to believe the unbelievable. "Observation?!" she asks, incredulous. She reminds him that he was barely competitive in the Fallen Comrades competition, perhaps the ultimate test of observation. Rich has no answer, is permitted no answer, but the tone has changed. The jurors, who all fell due to the Tagi conspiracy perpetrated by Rich—and joined by Kelly—are becoming adversarial.

Now it's Sue's turn. Sue is pensive as she stands, plants her feet, and stares hard across the fire at Kelly and Rich. When she speaks, her tone is reasoned but tight, like she's addressing a crowded court. What follows

Colleen

is a speech that will live in the annals of television history. "Um…" she begins, "I have no questions, I just have statements.

"Rich, you're a very openly arrogant, pompous human being, but I admire your frankness with it. You have worked hard to get where you're at, and you started working hard way before you came to the island. So with my work ethic background, I give that credit to you. But, on the other hand, your inability to admit your failures without going into a whiny speech makes you a bit of a loser in life.

"Kelly, the rafting persona queen, you did get stomped on, on national TV, by a city boy that never swam—let alone been in the woods or jungle or been on a boat in his life. You sucked on that game. Anyways, I was your friend at the beginning of this, really thinking that you were a true friend. I was willing to be sitting there and put you next to me—at that time you were sweeter than me, I'm not a very openly nice person, I'm just frank, forward, and telling it the way it is—

Greg

"To have you sit there next to me and me lose $900,000 dollars just to stomp on somebody like this [*motions to Richard*]. But as the game went along and the two tribes merged, you lied to me, which showed me the true person that you are. You're very two-faced and manipulative to get where you're at anywhere in life, that's why you fail all the time. So at that time of the game, I decided just to go out with my alliance to my family, and just to hold my dignity and values in check and hope I hadn't lost too many of them and...uh...play the game just as long as possible and hang in there as long as possible.

"But Kelly, go back to a couple times Jeff said to you, 'What goes around comes around.' It's here. You will not get my vote. My vote will go to Richard, and I hope that is the one vote that makes you lose the money. If it's not, so be it. I'll shake your hand and I'll go on from here, but if I was ever to pass you along in life again and you were lying there dying of thirst, I would not give you a drink of water. I would let the vultures take you and do whatever they want with you, with no ill regrets.

"I plead to the jury tonight to think a little bit about the island that we have been on. This island is pretty much full of only two things: snakes and rats. And in the end with Mother Nature we have Richard the snake, who knowingly went after prey, and Kelly, who turned into the rat that ran around like the rats do on this island, trying to run from the snake. I feel we owe it to the island's spirits that we've come to know to let it be, in the end, the way Mother Nature intended it to be—for the snake to eat the rat."

Dirk

Those in attendance will never forget the moment. The sense of astonishment is incredible. Everyone knew Sue was capable of such rage—such bile—but to witness such a pointed attack is intense. It is hard to look at Kelly. She's a proud woman, and more defiant than she has admitted. For her to sit there and take it must be so difficult, especially

B.B.

when she has similar emotions about Sue. Even Rich is amazed.

Finally, Greg gets up. He's been smoking a lot since being voted off, and smells like tobacco. He's also been strangely quiet, and his sly wit is nowhere in evidence. But leave it to Greg to add a touch of whimsy to the proceedings. "Pick a number between one and ten," he orders each castaway. There will be no logic to his voting, other than which castaway comes closer to the number in his mind. Rich picks seven. Kelly, three.

Both Rich and Kelly are given a chance to make final remarks. That should be a grand moment for both of them, a chance to tell the world what they're all about. But compared with Sue's oration, theirs pale.

The ebb and flow of all great drama revolves around pacing. Probst knows there is no better time to bring Tribal Council proceedings—and *Survivor*—to an end. "Time to vote," he says, standing and smacking his palms against the sides of his thighs. "You first," he says, pointing to Gervase.

One by one, the members of the jury get up and cast their votes. For the first time in *Survivor,* they are not voting someone off, but voting for a winner. The name they write on the ballots will win a million dollars.

In the end, the vote is 4 to 3 with Greg's "pick a number" effectively giving Rich the million dollars. He feigns shock, but it looks as if he knew all along that he would win. And, of course, he did. He'd said so months before flying to Pulau Tiga.

Wrap Party

*S*urvivor filming has concluded. The generators are back on and the island is hopping. It's a Pulau Tiga wrap party, a raucous island bash that makes a Jimmy Buffett concert look like a first-grade piano recital. The island has been home, prison, paradise, workplace, and sanctuary for the cast and crew (the crew especially; many have been on the island almost four months), and the sense of relief that it's all come to an end is as tangible as the smoky-sweet smell of barbecue wafting across the jungle clearing. Dance music pulses through the warm air.

With the exception of Gretchen, Sonja, Dirk, and B.B., every castaway is in attendance. The crew have seen the jury members on a regular basis over the past three weeks, but are surprised to see Stacey, Ramona, and Joel again. They are greeted like long lost friends, and told how much healthier they look since they've had a few good meals.

Probst has saved a bottle of champagne for the occasion. He passes it to me for a sip. Then Probst takes a long gulp, gives the bottle away, and goes to bed. Probst has a 6:00 A.M. boat back to KK and a flight from KK home to Los Angeles at 11:00. Preparation for the final Tribal Council has kept him from packing. He will be up another couple of hours, listening to the Howard Stern tapes a buddy sent from home, his personal luxury item since arriving on the island.

I walk away from the party and out along our newly constructed boat ramp. This is where demobilization of all our gear will begin in a few hours. The music softens as I walk, and soon I am alone with my thoughts and the tropical night sky. We have pulled off the impossible. The show is going to be exactly as I've dreamed. I thank the heavens for every break I've been given. After an hour or so I slowly walk back to the party.

Sue is holding court at the *Survivor* Bar, a line of Heinekens brought by admirers backed up on the polished ironwood surface. Her stories are bawdy, hilarious. Sue has a natural charisma that she's kept under wraps as part of her *Survivor* strategy, but now it's on display for all to see. Plus, the Tribal Council speech has taken a visible weight off her shoulders.

Kelly keeps to herself, chatting with members of the crew. Her deep friendship with Sue early in the show meant she had no other close acquaintances on the island. So she stays away from the castaways, and looks visibly stunned that she lost.

Rudy's having the time of his life. When the music is turned down, I step onstage to say a few words. Once I am finished, the chant goes up from the crowd: "Ru-dy, Ru-dy, Ru-dy..." Muted at first, the chant soon reverberates across the party, until a hundred voices are chanting for the curmudgeonly retiree to step up to the stage. When Rudy finally climbs up, a cheer sweeps through the crowd. I hand him the mike. Rudy, who hasn't said more than a sentence or two at a time in his entire stay on Pulau Tiga, turns out to be a natural showman. He tells two long jokes, both in very poor taste, very politically incorrect, and very funny. Both times he arrives at the punch line and the audience gasps, never imagining Rudy could tell those jokes anywhere but the hold of a warship. Then the laughter rocks through the crowd. Rudy's audacity, after

Ramona

Stacey

all, is why they brought him to the stage. He knows this and is playing to the crowd. This is just another example of Rudy being underestimated, then shocking people with the depth of his homespun intellect.

It's also another example of the production team concealing the true winner, for only very essential crew were present as Richard was voted the million-dollar winner. Having Rudy up onstage is a tacit way of suggesting he's the winner. There's no actual lying involved—I never actually claim that Rudy won—but then, it's not necessary. (Three months later, this bit of disinformation would pay off. *Good Morning America* would send a reporter to Pulau Tiga to play the part of spoiler: his job was to find out who won *Survivor*. He showed pictures of the final group of castaways to a number of Malaysians working on the island. Each one looked at Rudy's picture and pointed to him as the winner.)

The crowd's adoration and Rudy's obvious surprise and happiness that he's so loved is enough to convince the uninformed that Rudy is the winner. Especially when Richard looks so fatigued and eager to slip away, and Kelly is so unhappy.

The party goes on through the night. Sunrise finds Sue leaning on the *Survivor* Bar, still basking in the glow of her speech. It has been a hit with all those who saw it. Despite the sun's appearance, Sue's audience has grown, as has the line of proffered beers.

Richard, the winner, has been briefed on how to behave and what he can discuss about his victory with people at the party (nothing). After a brief appearance to eat, he disappears from the party after asking which bungalow he's to be sleeping in because he needs to take a shower. The next morning, even as Jenna and Gervase stroll on the beach after staying up all night, Rich will be down on the docks looking for a boat ride back to KK. He is showered and dressed in clean clothes that he hasn't worn since coming to the island. They hang on him, for he has lost thirty pounds on Pulau Tiga.

The boat carrying Probst will be full, but Richard cadges room on a second boat leaving moments later. By the time he arrives in KK and checks into the Magellan Sutera, a full-scale search has begun for him on Pulau Tiga. Producers never gave Richard clearance to leave the island, he voted himself off.

Countdown to a Hit

Before there was time to revel in successfully finishing filming or to dread the hard months of editing ahead, *Survivor* was dealt a crushing blow: Richard Hatch had been arrested on child abuse charges. Rhode Island police claimed he dragged his son from bed at 4:00 A.M. to go jogging because Richard was so pleased with his island weight loss that his son's accompanying weight gain was a sore spot.

The charges were later dropped. Richard denied the allegations and even filed legal action to refurbish his tarnished reputation, but that last week of April was a hard time to be associated with CBS or the *Survivor* production. The worst thing that could happen—*Survivor* winner arrested, child abuse—came to pass. It was very likely the police investigation and subsequent media scrutiny would leak The Secret.

That single event changed the way the *Survivor* production crew viewed the show. Being alone on a deserted tropical island, even when taking active steps to insure secrecy, it's easy to slip into the secure feeling that nothing will go wrong. On an island, it's easy to monitor every member of the population. The Secret was safe on the island, and we assumed it would be relatively easy to slip back into America and monitor the situation. But Richard's arrest changed all that. His name was on television nationwide, on the wire services, and all over the Internet. Already, a core group of men and women had taken an interest in the show and were dying to know The Secret. Richard had been briefed by CBS on how to behave publicly—no expensive purchases, no change in lifestyle. These were things a good investigative reporter would watch the castaways for as a means of finding out who won. Richard's sole task was to avoid drawing attention to himself.

The most daunting prospect of all was the realization that the final episode of *Survivor* wasn't set to air for almost four months. In that time, more and more people would have to learn the winner's name. A whole new group of tape loggers, editors, composers, and production assistants would be flooding the *Survivor* office to conduct the mammoth task of preparing thirteen episodes.

It seemed like The Secret would be impossible to keep.

In a strange way, though, Richard's arrest raised public awareness of the show. It's been said that there's no such thing as bad publicity, and this was proving true. As we counted down to the May 31 air-

Gervase

ing of the first show, it seemed that media attention began to slowly focus on its debut.

Summer shows are supposed to be filler, the sort of thing a network airs as an afterthought. The rationale is that summer is when families interrupt their normal viewing habits to take vacations, go to ball games, and simply spend more time outdoors during the longer days. Slating *Survivor* as a summer show was a good way for CBS to air the show with little risk. First, since every second of commercial time had been sold before the show went into production (and at relatively low prices), the show was already profitable. If *Survivor* tanked, CBS would be none the poorer.

The second reason CBS was wise to run *Survivor* in the summer was reduced expectation. If it failed, the blame could be placed on summer scheduling. *Survivor* was, after all, a reality show. And reality shows had taken a big credibility hit after *Who Wants to Marry a Multimillionaire* aired on Fox. If *Survivor* failed, it would ring the death knell for reality shows. So it was, to a great extent, an experiment.

But as the days counted down to the first episode, *Survivor*'s media awareness continued to grow. It helped that there was little else on television in May. One by one, the major network television shows aired their season finales. Attention ceased to focus on whether Carol Hathaway would reunite with Doug Ross on *ER* and how Michael J. Fox would leave *Spin City*. It focused, instead, on *Survivor*. Richard Hatch's arrest had quietly faded from the limelight, so he was hardly the source of the curiosity. People across America were anticipating the show because they were curious about how sixteen crazy people would spend thirty-nine days on a deserted tropical island.

In mid-May, I was sitting in my office conducting a staff meeting when the phone rang. CBS was calling to tell me that ABC was rescheduling the phenomenally successful *Who Wants to Be a Millionaire* head-to-head with *Survivor*. I was stunned. *Millionaire* was a giant-killer, single-handedly vaulting ABC to the top of the ratings, crushing any show aired against it. Putting *Millionaire* opposite *Survivor* could kill our show before it got a chance to find an audience. My fear was that if people didn't tune in to our first episode, they wouldn't tune in at all, thinking they'd missed too much to catch up.

I put the phone back in the cradle, leaned my elbows on my desk, and spoke in hushed tones, "ABC just scheduled *Millionaire* against us." Then I realized something...

...And I said in a confident voice, "Good, we can't lose. If they beat us, no one will be surprised, but if we come close to them, or even beat them, it will be a disaster for ABC. All the pressure is on *Millionaire*. We can relax a little."

I knew that *Millionaire* was looking tired. Ratings had been leveling off. Maybe there was hope. My good friend Michael Davies, executive producer of *Millionaire*, called me later that day to "wish me luck." I knew he had nothing to do with this scheduling decision and I heard in his voice that he didn't like it. Michael is extremely smart and saw no value in going head-to-head. There was no upside for him.

The Premiere

CBS had been airing promos for two weeks, squeezing tight images of island life into five-, fifteen-, and thirty-second spots. The castaways' faces flashed on the screen along with images of lunging sea kraits and other visuals designed to show the severity of island life.

The term "overnight success" is used so often that it's lost its power. But that's what *Survivor* was. Overall, *Millionaire* beat us that first night, although in some demographics we edged out Regis and his contestants by the narrowest of margins.

The American public, however, cared little for all that. What was important was their sudden fascination with island life. People everywhere debated whether it was fair or not to vote poor Sonja off the island. It was seen as such a heartless way to deal with such a sweet old lady. The cry of ageism began sounding, but the show was about survival. Would Sonja have survived in that environment? Clearly not. Besides, the ageism demonstrators had no idea their argument had no legs. Rudy, the oldest castaway of all, would almost go the distance. There was no ageism, just hard reality. Or, as we said on Pulau Tiga, dramality—that convergence of drama and reality.

People began saying the phrase that would be repeated all summer: "I don't care who wins, as long as it's not that gay guy." Richard was the nation's favorite villain since *Dallas*'s J.R.

Survivor was a watercooler show, meaning it was the broadcast everyone talked about at work the following day, creating tremendous word of mouth.

Survivor phrases began springing into the public lexicon in the week between the first and second show. Ahead-of-the-curve hipsters were saying "Don't vote me off" and "It's time for you to go," making *Survivor* awareness cool. The CBS website, which contained behind-the-scenes information about island life, was on its way to becoming the most popular entertainment website in history. It received so many hits the night of the first show that its server was overwhelmed, and the site crashed.

Sonja

After we trounced *Millionaire* in Week Three, it was clear *Survivor* owned a growing audience. In fact, the numbers grew and grew through the summer, and *Millionaire*'s time slot was moved after the first *Survivor* episodes. They leveled off after the fourth episode, but leapt again two weeks later. The other networks had ceased programming anything substantial opposite us. We had become a juggernaut. When *Survivor*'s former castaways appeared on CBS's *The Early Show* after being voted off, its ratings spiked. When they appeared on *The Late Show with David Letterman* that same night, his show saw the same spike.

The nation embraced our little island experience. Actors like Bruce Willis and Ray Romano were fans. Other celebrity fans included Debra Messing *(Will & Grace)*, Eddie Van Halen, and Valerie Bertinelli. Will Smith's company even contacted Gerv for an audition. The 2000 presidential campaign was sprinkled with rhetoric about voting people off. The tabloids began contacting *Survivor* crew members, offering cash (confidentially) for the winner's name. One crew member even had his email hacked, so a quiet warning went out to *Survivor* personnel to avoid discussing the winner or each episode's results over email. Non-sanctioned websites sprung up, theorizing about the eventual Survivor. Chat rooms were dedicated to talks of the best and worst castaways, and it seemed everybody had a favorite—even Richard had his backers.

Then things began to get weird. Fanatics were taping the show and watching it frame by frame, hoping for subtle clues about the eventual winner, or even just future episodes. Savvy viewers noted that a shot of Rudy during the opening segment showed him with a beard, leading many to believe he would be around awhile.

Ramona mentioned, when asked by a television interviewer her thoughts on fellow castaways, that Gretchen was a "true survivor." This was seen as a faux pas of the highest variety, and rumors began circulating that CBS was filing a $4 million breach of contract suit against Ramona. As was their policy throughout the *Survivor* summer, CBS's publicity department would neither confirm nor deny any rumors.

When Sean mentioned in an interview that he'd spend another thirty days on the island, many realized Sean had lasted well into the game, too. It went on and on. It's worth pointing out that none of the viewers noticed a split-second image during one opening credit sequence: a distant, backlit shot of a man holding a torch on Bird Island. The shot was taken at sunset, and the man's face is obscured by distance, but the torso is clearly that of the ultimate winner—Richard.

Hackers were rumored to have cracked the CBS website. One claimed to have discovered a panel showing each castaway's photograph. Each had an X over their face—except Gervase. The hacker posted his discovery on the web, and soon newspapers and television programs all across America were sure Gervase had won. *USA Today* polled a cross section of Americans about who they thought might be the final Survivor. The answer: Gerv, at even odds. There was a mild uproar as Americans wondered if being charming and

Sean

lazy was really the mode for achieving true Survivorship. The answer came a few weeks later when Gerv was voted off. America's collective gasp (of relief and confusion) punctuated a new level of *Survivor*. The game had spilled into American households—not just through TV sets, but through hearts and minds—as people realized that a cat and mouse game between CBS and those wishing to prematurely unveil "The Survivor Secret" had begun. Questions were asked about whether we were behind the hacking. Again, we would neither confirm nor deny that the "Gervase X" was a hoax.

That won't happen here, either (hey guys, we've got another game to play). Let's just say we were passive about the hackers' attentiveness at first, but as they got more active and determined to predict the winner, we upped the ante.

Meanwhile, the *Survivor* production office hummed with activity. We were busier than ever, trying to increase the quality of the shows and structure the dramality in such a way that the American public didn't get bored or see the show as formulaic.

All that work paid off as the ratings kept rolling in. Then CBS gave us the highest compliment of all, green-lighting *Survivor: The Australian Outback*. Immediately, commercials began airing during the show, and applications became available on the website. While the rest of America didn't know the conclusion of *Survivor: Borneo*, we were already back to square one, searching for candidates for a second, even better show.

Casting *Survivor: The Australian Outback*

Over forty-nine thousand people across America applied to be contestants on *Survivor: The Australian Outback.* They filled out applications on cbs.com and clipped them to homemade videotapes. Some mailed their packets attached to stuffed kangaroos or koala bears. One application was mailed with a large footlocker full of rubberized creepy crawlers. From those applications, a lucky eight hundred got to meet with casting personnel who traveled to sixteen cities around the country to interview the applicants in person. These were the eight hundred semifinalists.

This field was whittled to a final forty-eight. In early September, shortly after Sue Hawk's speech and Richard Hatch's victory were revealed (to another, much larger, collective national gasp) before 52 million people, one of the largest viewing audiences in television history, these forty-eight finalists were invited to Los Angeles for an intensive two weeks of interviews. In addition to *Survivor's* producers and casting team, CBS executives and host Jeff Probst were in attendance (psychiatrist Dr. Richard Levak and medical doctor Adrian Cohen administered psychological and medical testing in a separate section). Potential contestants were grilled relentlessly. No question—none!—was off limits: sex, drugs, you name it. The answers were revealing in their complexity, and as a marker of how badly the final forty-eight wanted to be Survivors. Needless to say, confidentiality was the order of the day.

When the final sixteen were chosen during the last week of September, plans were immediately hatched to smuggle them out of America and into Australia when the time came to travel. The Internet was already rife with speculation about *Survivor: The Australian Outback,* both the cast and location. All that interest was a healthy, wonderful thing. But just like opening a Christmas present a month early, the surprise of *Survivor* would be deflated if the contestants' names and the show's location became public knowledge before we decided it was time.

Close cooperation between American and Australian officials allowed the final sixteen to fly under assumed names. They carried their own passports and flew on the same aircraft (sitting separately, of course, and with a chaperone to ensure there was no conversation or communication of any kind with fellow contestants), enduring the sixteen-hour flight to Australia, passage through customs in Sydney, and a three-hour regional flight from Sydney to Cairns. The contestants were immediately transferred to a small private plane and whisked to a secret pre-outback briefing location. Not only was no one's identity discovered, not a single contestant was questioned about whether or not they were with the show.

With Australia still buzzing from the recently completed Sydney Olympics, it seems only right, as I begin to watch the drama unfold—the contestants' panic as they start a new life, the confusion of being thrust into a tribe with people who will decide their fate, the look of apprehension as they survey the outback's desolation—to smile and say softly, "Let the games begin."

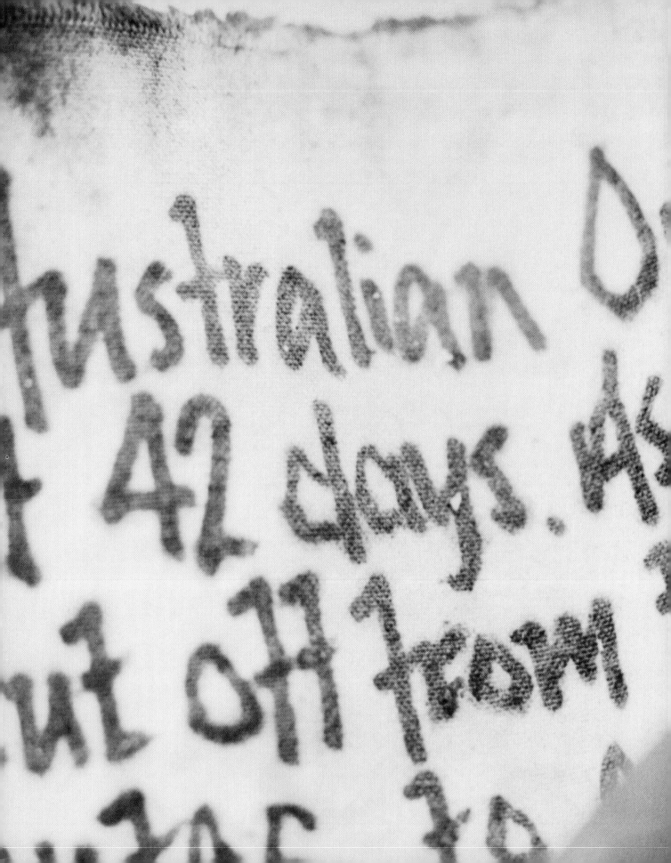

Chapter Two

A Short History of the Land Down Under

Why Australia?

Trying to define Australia in a few simple sentences is no easier than trying to do the same about America. There is too much complexity, too much contrast for easy characterization. Australia is an island, nation, and continent, a claim no other place on earth can make. Her landscape's character is epic, enigmatic, dangerous. Australia is big, roughly four-fifths the size of Canada, but the national personality is that of the underdog. Evocative, sprawling place names like Eighty Mile Beach, the Great Sandy Desert, and Lake Disappointment are the norm instead of the exception on her maps. The populace affects a British heritage, but has a much more enduring connection with China and Vietnam. And, due to their southern hemisphere seasons, the notion of a white Christmas strikes Aussies as absurd as, well, snow on the Fourth of July.

In short, this world turned upside down is an ideal setting for the second edition of *Survivor.*

The decision to shoot *Survivor* in Australia was made in early April 2000, even as filming was underway on Pulau Tiga. To be proactive, it was important to choose the second location early in case *Survivor* became a hit. There were several reasons for this: first, filming of the second edition would have to begin just a few short months after the first edition wrapped. That meant logistical realities such as local approval, site security, transportation, and the like would have to be handled immediately. Typically, those elements are the most time-consuming; the sooner they could be concluded, the better.

Second, having a second site selected would make it easier for the *Survivor* production team to set aside that task and focus on the day-to-day minutiae of preparation—selecting contestants and camera crews, preparing budgets.

Finally, if *Survivor* turned out to be a hit, finding a location for the second show without creating a media frenzy would be virtually impossible. The travels of *Survivor* location scouts would be a very

Arriving in the outback

difficult secret to keep. Because of the risk of those individuals being discovered in their cloak-and-dagger travel or in similarly stealthy local negotiations, selecting a location early seemed wise.

A *Survivor* location has to be special. It must be evocative, transporting the armchair adventurer into the realm of fantasy, making them wish they were there. Nothing about a *Survivor* location should be mundane. No suggestion of the real world is allowed. Pulau Tiga, with its dangerous jungles and snake-infested surrounding waters, was such a place. What man or woman in modern society hasn't looked inside themselves and wondered if they could survive on a deserted island? What amenities would they require? Could they find food? Would isolation be intolerable or liberating?

The second location had to be just as intriguing, but in a different way. The premise would be survival after a failed expedition. The contestants would be the modern-day versions of Captain Cook's *Endeavour* crew, who were abandoned in the same area two hundred years ago. As with Cook and his men, *Survivor*'s contestants will be flung onto Australian shores, forced to carve out a living amid grave danger. This party of sixteen hardy adventurers is stranded in the wilds. They are on an island, just like the men and women of Pulau Tiga, but not an island surrounded by water. Instead, it is an island surrounded by harsh wilderness—unforgiving bush lands, thundering waterfalls, vast eucalyptus forests. If anything, the second edition of *Survivor* would be filmed in a locale more daunting and life-challenging than the first. It wouldn't be enough to match Pulau Tiga's hardships—the hardships must be surpassed.

True, *Survivor* is more about social survival than physical survival. But the pressure cooker of social survival is infinitely more daunting when hunger, fatigue, and danger are tangible and omnipresent. People break, emotionally and physically, under those circumstances. They do strange things, forge strange alliances—they act like Survivors.

So, in one of those impulsive gut decisions that I often make, Australia was chosen. I was familiar with Australia, having spent months there in 1997 producing *Eco-Challenge.* I knew firsthand that Australia has some of the world's most deadly wilderness. Not only are climatic conditions harsh, but the copious presence of poisonous snakes, poisonous spiders, and freshwater crocodiles ("freshies" in local parlance) surpassed even Pulau Tiga's nasties. And if all that wasn't enough, great white sharks and saltwater crocodiles whizzed about the Great Barrier Reef, ready to devour anything and everything silly enough to swim in their waters. No nation on earth is home to a more prehistoric collection of predators. I had no doubt that Australia would provide the ideal setting for *Survivor II.*

But where in Australia? The entire nation is a *Survivor* location scout's paradise. Should the contestants be flung into the mountainous Great Dividing Range along the eastern edge of the nation? Into the vast, red-rocked desert? Along the Great Barrier Reef? On one of those myriad tropical islands of pure white sand, where contestants would share living space with fifteen-foot saltwater crocodiles come ashore to sun? Or maybe in the barren northwest corner of Australia with its primitive lunar landscape?

Each of those locations was viable, but not nearly tough enough. I wanted it all—the mountains, the desert, the jungles, the beaches. What I had in mind was the state of Queensland, that tropical reach of Australia covering its northeast shoulder, bordered on one side by the Great Barrier Reef, split in two by the Great Diving Range, covered with harsh desert and deadly rain forest. The desert/jungle terrain of Queensland is like no other environment on earth. At fifty million years old, the rain forest of Queensland is the oldest on

earth—over thirty million years more mature than the Amazon. Unlike the smooth wet jungles of Pulau Tiga, Queensland's terrain is a dense, rocky affair. Often, patches of jungle exist side by side with the red clay desert, making for an enigmatic appearance much like the African savannah. Or the jungle might give way to eucalyptus forests that stretch miles and miles before congealing into jungle again. Waterfalls several hundred feet high and gorges narrow and tall appear out of nowhere. Just as *Survivor* regularly asks America to rethink their notion of survival, Queensland asks armchair adventurers to redefine their notion of "rain forest" and "desert," for what the viewers see fits into no neat category.

Australia from outer space

By the middle of May 2000, two weeks before the first episode of *Survivor* aired, I reached an arrangement with officials in Queensland to make it the official home of *Survivor*'s second edition. The forbidden section of Queensland—the area the Survivors will call home, and where they will vie for a million dollars—goes by a single name: outback. The very name implies deprivation and struggle. Why Australia? The answer can be found in that single word.

A Nation with a Castaway Past

Australia is a country with a vast castaway tradition. Until *Survivor II* begins shooting, the most famous castaway in Australian history is Lieutenant (later Captain) James Cook. After nearly sinking his vessel, the *Endeavour* (discovering the Great Barrier Reef in the process), Cook and his crew were marooned on Australian shores for almost three months. They very nearly stayed there forever.

Cook had been at sea for almost two years on an around-the-world journey and was making his way back to Great Britain. Along the way, he was charting the coast of eastern Australia. Beginning down in what is now the Bass Strait, he'd spent two months at the task and was almost done.

For all his detailed charting, recording every bend and spur of Australia's demanding shore, Cook was totally unaware that he was deep inside the Great Barrier Reef. This was understandable, given that this vast coral outcropping doesn't run parallel to the Australian coast. Rather, it angles toward the continent. In the south, the Great

Barrier Reef is hundreds of miles offshore, but in the far north—Cook's position—the reef and shore are almost one. Cook had unwittingly sailed between them, from which escape would be a supreme navigational feat. Not only does the Great Barrier Reef veer toward the coast as a single line, sections in the north sprout from the seabed like islands unto themselves. Cook would have to dodge these coral islands, for just one brush of razor-sharp coral against his wooden hull could prove calamitous.

On June 11, Cook noted several low-lying islands. Not having discovered the Great Barrier Reef yet, Cook supposed that they were specks of land. At eleven o'clock that night, content that the islands proved no danger to the *Endeavour*, Cook retired to his small cabin. No sooner had he stretched out in his swinging hammock than a tremendous crash thundered through the vessel. She came to a complete stop. Dressing quickly, Cook raced on deck to learn that the *Endeavour* was stuck fast on the Great Barrier Reef. The Australian coast lay ten miles away. A massive hole had been torn in the *Endeavour*'s hull and three feet of water already filled the lower decks.

"Scarce were we warm in our beds," wrote botanist Joseph Banks, a passenger on that journey, "when we were called up with the alarming news of the ship being fast ashore on a rock, which she in a few moments convinced us by beating very violently against the rocks. Our situation now became greatly alarming…we were little less than certain that we were upon sunken coral rocks, the most dreadful of all others on account of their sharp points and grinding quality, which cut through a ship's bottom almost immediately."

Cook acted quickly. The ninety-four-man crew was put to work pumping water from the hold. Fifty tons of non-vital supplies, including several cannons, were tossed overboard to lighten the ship. Then, as if placing a large Band-aid on the *Endeavour*'s wound, Cook ordered a spare sail to be wrapped around the outside of the ship, directly over the hole. Finally, after twenty-three hours of intensive labor, the *Endeavour* maneuvered away from the Great Barrier Reef. She limped toward shore, where Cook hoped to find wood and other supplies to repair his broken ship. Unlike other great expeditions, Cook's journey involved one vessel instead of two. Either Cook found a way to fix the gaping wound in the *Endeavour,* or he and his men would be stranded in Australia forever.

The *Endeavour* landed in what is now Cooktown, Queensland. The land was not inviting. "I climbed upon one of the highest hills over the harbor," he wrote of his first extended gaze at Australia. "It afforded a perfect view of the inlet, river, and adjacent country. The

land presented a very indifferent prospect. The lowlands near the river are all over with mangroves. Salt water flows in at every tide, and high lands appear barren and stoney."

A few days later, the strange country got even weirder. "This morning I saw an animal of a light mouse color and the full size of a greyhound, with a long tail like a greyhound's. In short, I should have taken it for a wild dog. But when walking or running it jumped like a hare or deer," Cook wrote of his first kangaroo sighting.

Cook was relieved to find plenty of supplies for fixing his vessel. The *Endeavour* was steered onto the beach, her contents were emptied out, and she was tilted onto her side so the ship's carpenters could do their work. The men—or The People, as Cook called his crew—lived in tents while their ship was being fixed.

There are symbolic parallels between Cook and *Survivor*. As the crow flies, Cook camped just a hundred miles from the *Survivor* location. The crew of *Survivor* (not the contestants; they will build their own shelters) are spending their months on location living in tents. Both crews suffered the persistence and ubiquity of Australia's mosquito and fly populations. Both saw firsthand the abundance of wildlife—wombats, kangaroos, kookaburras—populating Australia. Unlike Cook, however, who enjoyed the relatively dry and mild

AUSTRALIAN ODDS AND ENDS

Official Name: *Commonwealth of Australia*

Capital: *Canberra*

Population: *approximately twenty million*

Size: *2,978,145 square miles*

Number of States: *Seven (New South Wales, Tasmania, Queensland, Victoria, Northern Territory, Southern Australia, Western Australia)*

Popular Nickname: *Oz*

Length of the Great Barrier Reef: *1,250 miles (roughly the distance from Boston to Miami)*

Of World's Ten Most Poisonous Species of Snakes, Number Residing in Australia: *eight*

weather of Australia's winter months, *Survivor*'s crew will be filming during the wet, hot summer.

Cook would remain on the shores of Cooktown two months. In that time, he and his men became the first Europeans to experience Queensland's peculiar charms. Until then, saltwater crocodiles, great white sharks, and kangaroos were unknown beyond Australia. When the time came to set sail, the *Endeavour* weaved carefully out of the Great Barrier Reef (very nearly running aground again), turned left at the Torres Strait, and was home a year later. Though Cook made two other voyages of circumnavigation, he never returned to Australia. Her rugged beauty fascinated him, but Australia was too complex for easy exploration. "It was with great regret that I was obliged to quit this coast," he wrote as Australia disappeared over the horizon on August 14, 1770.

A Little Dose of Australian History

Despite—or perhaps, because of—his calamitous introduction to life in Australia, modern-day Australians celebrate Cook as their discoverer. In actuality, he came to the game rather late. Some forty thousand years ago, a land bridge extended down from Vietnam, through Indonesia and Borneo (though Pulau Tiga was still underwater then), and into Australia. The forebearers of Australia's Aborigine population trekked down along that bridge, populating Australia all the way down to the bridge's end at the southern coast of what is now Tasmania. Once the land bridge was covered by rising waters at the end of the last ice age, Australia belonged exclusively to the nomadic Aborigines.

Today, Australia is almost entirely desert and arid land in the middle of the country, with the outer perimeter more lush and habitable. Think of a monk's haircut—bald in the middle and fringed by hair—but the bald spot in the middle is three thousand miles across. This explains why the overwhelming majority of Australia's population live in the outer perimeter, along the ocean.

However, Australia wasn't always synonymous with dry heat. When the Aborigines first arrived, they found a lush, dense land populated by such oddities as ten-foot-tall kangaroos. They proceeded to build a thriving civilization. The complexity of their achievements has long been overlooked in favor of the more glamorous cultures of the Incas and Egyptians. But long before the Egyptians built the pyramids, the Aborigines were practicing ritual burial. They drew ornate petroglyphs, using a distinct form of drawing and interpretive storytelling that survives today. They were accomplished hunters, fashioning spears and axes to kill those fierce kangaroos—and the much more fierce crocodile population.

The first Europeans mistook the Aborigines for simple savages. Their skin was black from the fierce Australian sun, unlike the lighter-colored Pacific Islanders the Europeans were used to, and the Aboriginal bent toward minimal clothing and long walks of self-discovery ("walkabouts") struck the Europeans as primitive. That point of view had a lasting impression. As with Native Americans in the United States, the Aborigine people were systematically subjugated in Australia. Their culture was stamped out and their beliefs ridiculed. Aboriginal children were even taken from their parents and raised by white families in order to discourage the propagation of Aboriginal ways. Aboriginal land was taken away by white settlers, especially in Queensland during the Palmer River gold rush of 1873.

Not that the Aborigines accepted the domination passively. Their population at the time of European settlement was over three hundred thousand, greatly outnumbering whites. Homesteaders routinely fell victim to Aborigine spears. Explorers attempting to push into the heart of Australia routinely clashed with Aborigines. When explorer Edward Eyre tried to cross the continent in 1840, his partner Baxter was killed by their Aborigine guides. Eyre escaped to the coast, but the expedition was abandoned. In 1848 Edmund Kennedy attempted a trek through Queensland's rain forest. Nine of the thirteen members of his party died, with Kennedy among those on the receiving end of an Aborigine spear. However, Britain's refusal to accept Aborigine ownership of the land (the continent was

categorized *terra nullius*—belonging to no one) encouraged pioneer settlements. The homesteaders took control of the land with guns and determination. The European introduction of stock animals such as pigs, sheep, and cattle further undercut the Aborigine way of life by destroying the land and eradicating many forms of native wildlife. Because killing an Aborigine wasn't against the law, Europeans retaliated viciously when their sheep and cattle were slaughtered by Aboriginal guerrilla raiding parties. Aboriginal warlords such as Yagan, Jandamarra, and Nemarlurk were notorious among the Europeans for their brilliant battle plans and stealth. Their weapons were superior to the European flintlock rifle colonists used, until the introduction of the repeating rifle in the 1870s. Those Aborigines that didn't retreat into the heart of the nation were either assimilated as second-class citizens or died of European diseases such as smallpox and venereal disease.

It wasn't until the 1920s that the Aborigine wars finally came to an end. The last bastions of militant Aborigines, located in northern and central Australia, ceased spearing pioneers. By then segregation was in place. Aborigines were prevented from buying or owning property. They were also prohibited from holding jobs. In 1918 the Aboriginals Ordinance allowed the state to remove Aboriginal children from their homes and institutionalize them or place them in foster homes.

Aborigines were formally given Australian citizenship in 1967, but it's only recently that reconciliation has occurred. Aboriginal children are now raised to appreciate their heritage. Appreciation for Aboriginal culture has become a part of Australian life. Archaeologists have discovered the elaborate remains of early Aboriginal life that prove they have long been a visionary, brilliant society. Aboriginal music and art have become celebrated in the process. The emotional lighting of the torch at the 2000 Olympic Games by Australian Cathy Freeman, an Aboriginal woman, and her subsequent victory in the women's 400-meter dash were seen by many Australians as an act of healing. As Freeman dashed down the home stretch in the 400, thousands of flashbulbs punctuated the night and almost every television in Australia was tuned in. The solidarity was complete as Freeman jogged a victory lap carrying the flag of Australia and that of the Aboriginal people.

Of course, an athletic event doesn't erase two centuries of mistrust between whites and Aborigines. But Australia is committed to healing. The Aboriginal ways—once misunderstood and lampooned—are being embraced as a vital part of the national heritage.

Aboriginal terms like "walkabout" and "billabong" have become a part of the Australian vocabulary. The mystical Aboriginal belief system, focused on nature and the mind, is no longer seen as heretical but as a source of intrigue.

It All Began with the Greeks

Long after the Aboriginal exodus across the land bridge and a relatively short time prior to Cook's extended stay via shipwreck, Australia's existence was the subject of considerable debate in Europe. Just as the depth and breadth of the heavens are unknown to modern man, so the oceans were in 500 B.C.E. and on through the sixteenth century. The search for Australia was that age's version of searching for life on other planets.

The controversy started five centuries before Christ's birth. The Greeks knew that, despite its flat appearance, the earth was round. If the earth was round, with the land masses of Africa and Europe dominating the northern hemisphere, then, the Greeks speculated, a land mass of equal size and heft was necessary at the bottom of the world—down under, if you will. The land mass was necessary to keep the world in balance and prevent it from twirling out of solar orbit. When Ptolemy drew the first comprehensive world map in C.E. 140, he stepped into this unknown realm by drawing in a monstrous continent located far to the south of Asia. Though this hunk of land was never located through the first millennium—not by Europeans, at least—Ptolemy's map was never questioned.

Roughly one thousand years ago, sailors from China and Indonesia began making annual forays to Australia to harvest sea cucumbers from its northern shores. Europe, however, was mired in the Dark Ages at the time. Navigational terms like "latitude" and "longitude" were centuries distant, as was the boom in world travel that would accompany them. Meanwhile, European cartographers—not having a name for the unknown continent—began referring to it as "Terra Incognita," unknown land. In 1570, cartographer Abraham Ortelius revised the name, drawing a new world map and calling the undiscovered land "Terra Australis Nondum Cognita." In 1814, explorer Matthew Flinders would shorten the name to simply "Australia" (southern land).

The first Europeans to find Australia did so by accident. In 1616, the Dutch vessel *Eendracht* was sailing east after rounding Africa, en route to the busy port of Batavia (now Jakarta). Strong winds blew her off course as she sailed through the Indian Ocean, shoving her far to the southeast instead of the more northerly course she was hoping for. The crew made land on what is now Australia's western coast. They dubbed this dirty, windblown stretch of land New Holland. Subsequent Dutch exploration charted the south, north, and west coasts of the new continent. Dutch skipper Abel Tasman discovered the region's southerly point and named it after the Dutch governor of Batavia, a man by the name of Van Diemen. Later, the name would be changed to honor the discoverer. Hence, Tasmania. An ironic footnote is that Tasman never set foot on this land. He was too cowed by the sight of hostile Aborigines on shore.

For a long while the Indian Ocean was a Dutch pond. Australia wasn't colonized and the interior wasn't charted. Then the British got involved in 1699. They turned to a most unlikely man to usher in their new age of exploration. William Dampier, a former pirate, requested and was granted command of the *Roebuck*, a British Royal Navy vessel. He was a swashbuckling man, and clashed repeatedly with the ship's officers who'd been sent along to keep an eye on him (one rigid lieutenant grated on Dampier so much that he eventually stranded the man in South America). After rounding the Cape of Good Hope on Africa's southern tip, Dampier boldly pushed the *Roebuck* off the shipping lanes in search of new lands. Like the Dutch a century before, he landed on Australia's west coast. Dampier had hoped to find gold but found little but sand. He returned home by way of South America and faced a court martial brought by the ship's officers. The charges effectively ended Dampier's career as an explorer. Soon thereafter, Dampier returned to piracy.

Dampier and the *Roebuck* accomplished very little, and found no

The states of Australia

Australian Slang

BANANA BENDER
resident of Queensland

BARBIE
barbecue

BILLABONG
water hole

BLOWIES
large flies

COBBER
friend, mate

DAKS
pants

DIDGERIDOO
native instrument

THE DRY
*The May–October dry season
in Northern Australia*

DUNNY
outhouse

FAIR DINKUM
honest

FAIR GO
to give someone a chance

G'DAY
hello, hey

GOOD ON YA
nice effort

JACKAROO
a young outback cowboy

JOURNO
journalist

KNACKERED
tired

LARRIKIN
a young punk

MOZZIES
mosquitoes

NEVER NEVER
the most remote region of the outback

NO WORRIES
that's O.K.

PISSED
drunk

RECKON
I agree with you

RIPPER
very good

TWO POT SCREAMER
someone who can't hold their liquor

ROOT
sexual intercourse

TINNY
a small can of beer

SALTIE
saltwater crocodile

THE WET
rainy season in northern Australia

SHARK BISCUIT
inexperienced surfer

WALKABOUT
a long solitary walk of self-discovery

SPARROW'S FART
daybreak

WOOP-WOOP
the outback

TALL POPPIES
overachievers

YAKKA
work

TALL POPPY SYNDROME
cutting an overachiever down to size

YOBBO
a jerk

new territory. But what made the voyage remarkable was what happened later. Dampier wrote a riveting—and largely fabricated—book about the journey, *Voyage to New Holland*.

The book became a bestseller (it was so well known that Jonathan Swift paid homage when he wrote *Gulliver's Travels* thirty years later, naming a character "Dampier"). Like a national family heirloom, *Voyage to New Holland* inspired one generation of explorers after another. The British began sending other voyagers to find the

land of riches Dampier chronicled. None succeeded. However, in 1768 Lieutenant James Cook, a tall, muscular man born of modest means with no previous experience in command, sailed from London aboard the *Endeavour*. His charter was to circumnavigate the globe, stopping first in Tahiti to observe the planet Venus's transit across the sun.

The assignment was, in effect, a suicide mission. The British admiralty (the navy's governing board) gave Cook explicit orders to sail from Tahiti due south into the uncharted waters of the Southern Ocean. These fierce seas are considered the most unpredictable on earth, prone to icebergs, one-hundred-foot waves, and hurricane-force winds. After sailing into these waters, Cook was to find the Great Southern Continent. Among his crew were naturalists to catalogue the new plants and animals he would find, and artists to draw these wonders.

Like Dampier before him, Cook was a loner. He was the first man in British naval history to climb all the way from the enlisted ranks to an officer's commission, then command. Born a farm boy, he talked with a country accent that set him apart from the polished London tones of blue-blooded officers. He was almost forty when the *Endeavour* sailed, an age at which most sailors of his era had either drowned or were considering retirement.

Yet Cook was more than up to the admiralty's task. He plunged from Tahiti into the Southern Ocean, then sailed to and fro searching for the missing continent. After a time he gave up and sailed east, then spent six months charting every nook and cove of New Zealand. He'd been at sea two years by then. No other explorer in history had been so reluctant to turn for home. But after New Zealand, Cook began the journey back to London. Taking one last stab at finding the Great Southern Continent, Cook remained in the high latitudes.

Which is how Cook stumbled into the eastern Australia coast. It wasn't the Great Southern Continent (that designation would go to Antarctica), but it was uncharted land. No European had been there before. Landing at a spot he named Botany Bay (contiguous to what is now Sydney International Airport) on April 27, 1770, Cook declared the land in the name of King George III, replenished his ship's stores, and proceeded northward up the coast. Along the way he named landmarks and islands. As Cook had been naming points around the globe for two years by the time he got to Australia, those he bestowed upon Australia were rather arcane (Hinchingbrook Island, for instance, is named for the estate of Lord Sandwich, Cook's patron) but many still remain. Five weeks after sailing from Botany Bay, Cook ran into that chunk of the Great Barrier Reef known today as Endeavour Reef.

After Cook repaired the *Endeavour* (alongside the Endeavour River) and sailed from Australian waters, no British vessel returned for almost a decade.

Working on the Chain Gang

Prior to the American Revolutionary War, the most hardened British criminals were shipped to prisons in Georgia and Florida. Two hundred offenses were punishable by death but many offenders were reprieved on the condition that they be transported abroad. However, the swamps, snakes, alligators, heat, and humidity were a sharp contrast to life in damp, cool Britain. Many prisoners regretted their decision for "transport," believing they had entered a colonial version of hell. The standard sentence was seven years hard labor, but the brutality (jailers, mostly Royal Marines, whipped inmates with cat-o'-nine-tails whose tendrils were flecked with bone, which dragged at the skin of a man's

bare back as he was beaten) and living conditions made for a high mortality rate. It was common knowledge that once a man set foot on the prison ship from England, his chances of returning were slim.

With the British on the losing end of the Revolutionary War, transport was ceased. Criminals were incarcerated in traditional British prisons. When those filled, ships deemed unfit to sail the high seas were stripped of their masts and turned into floating prisons. The Thames was lined with these fetid horrors. Eventually, there weren't enough ships to hold all the criminals. Britain found itself searching for a new prison colony. It had to be distant and hellish. Land had to be plentiful. Escape had to be futile; with any luck a series of natural predators would eat those unwise enough to try.

Enter Australia. In 1778, King George III, a pop-eyed man of German extraction, announced a plan for transporting convicts to the land Cook had discovered. Based on the recommendation of Sir Joseph Banks (the same Banks from Cook's *Endeavour*, and a man who compared the Aborigine unfavorably with cattle), the former unknown continent was chosen as a replacement. Banks told of alligators and snakes and spiders, and vast swampy tracts unsuited for farming but perfect for incarcerating men—an ideal prison.

It wasn't until January 26, 1788, that Captain Arthur Phillip, 736 convicts, and 294 others sailed into Botany Bay. Phillip, much to his surprise, discovered the French explorer La Perouse already at anchor. Even as Phillip was preparing to unload his scurvy-ridden human cargo (forty prisoners had died during the seven-month passage and were buried at sea), La Perouse was in the process of claiming Australia in the name of France. Sir Phillip, whose well-armed First Fleet greatly outnumbered La Perouse, chased the Frenchman away. Australia, after centuries of Chinese and Malays and Dutch, was British.

Sir Arthur Phillip got busy establishing the first prison. If he had any doubts that his new settlement was uncomfortably distant from Britain and in need of self-reliance, they were settled when the first supply ship from home went overdue. It had sunk off Africa. Phillip sent a message home asking for a shipment of non-prisoners with a knowledge of farming, but received only twenty such men in the first decade. Meanwhile, convoy upon convoy of prisoners arrived, sometimes a thousand men at a time. Necessity drove Phillip and his new colony to wean itself from Britain. The jailers and prisoners were becoming one.

In time Phillip moved north, searching for a better harbor and more advantageous fortifications than the low-lying mangroves of Botany Bay. What he found was a place Cook had merely sailed past,

a site that many consider the most perfect natural harbor on earth. The wind ranged hard outside its enormous basalt cliffs, but inside the massive harbor all was calm, protected. Phillip named the expanse Port Jackson and promptly built a settlement along its banks. Later the name was changed to honor a prominent Briton, Lord Sydney. The perfect natural harbor soon became Australia's most vital city and port. In time Phillip went back to England. His replacement as governor was William Bligh, best known as Captain Bligh of *Mutiny on the Bounty* fame.

By the mid-1800s, the transformation of Australia from prison colony to nation had begun. Some four hundred thousand acres in land grants had been dispersed to jailers, and the waterfront property once considered prime prison real estate was found to have great aesthetic value. Beautiful homes had begun lining the waterways of Sydney Harbor. Former prisoners began requesting and receiving land grants. The same men who had once made the grim journey from England to Australia as prisoners now stayed on after their sentences were complete, building the streets and bridges and homes of the exciting new land. It was a place where a man could reinvent himself; a place where anything could happen.

Once Sydney had been domesticated, the search began for another prison site. Ideally, the land would be so primitive and misbegotten that escape would be impossible for the prisoners and the land unattractive to potential settlers. Thus was Queensland colonized. In 1824, fifty-four years after Cook's departure, prisoners were sent to this rugged territory thousands of miles due north of Sydney.

All bets were off when gold was discovered in the mid-nineteenth century (ironically, at roughly the same time as the California gold rush). A massive land grab ensued. Settlers poured in and staked their claims. Gun battles were frequent. Cooktown, where Cook had beached the *Endeavour* for repairs, became the hub of this freewheeling new society. Over one hundred brothels and saloons lined the streets as men exhausted from months in the bush searching for gold came in to blow off steam. The town's population was over thirty thousand.

Britain had been trying to maintain control of Australia, but its power was slowly slipping away. When gold was discovered, that process was hastened. Thousands of Scots, Irish, and Brits shipped out to Australia in search of prosperity (Asians and Pacific Islanders were prohibited from entering the country). The nation's convict past was diluted by the millions of newcomers. On January 1, 1901, Australia formally became a nation unto itself. It remained a member of the British Commonwealth.

Chapter Three

The Playing Field

The Locale

Survivor: The Australian Outback will be held in an area of the outback surrounding the Herbert River. On one side, the Great Dividing Range lies between the contestants and the coast. On the other lies the outback, stretching into a red-rocked infinity. The landscape is bleak and vast, thoroughly underpopulated. The terrain is best described as a savannah—think of it as prairie with a scattering of eucalyptus, wattle, and native shrubs, and an ambient temperature that seems more suited to the fiery bowels of a steel mill.

As before, the contestants will be split into two tribes to start the game. They will live along the banks of the Upper Herbert, one of the hundreds of meandering outback rivers that seem to spring from nowhere and find their way to the Pacific. The beaches along the riverbank are gravel. The river is very wide and runs slowly where the tribal camps will be located. It's about one hundred feet from one side of the Herbert to the other. The distance between tribes is several miles, or about a four-hour trek. The gum trees along the bank are alive with the peal of kookaburras, cockatoos, and rainbow lorikeets. Crocodiles inhabit every deep water hole on the river. They're mainly seen at night, their red eyes casting a glow as they patrol along the billabongs. Families of dingoes and kangaroos come cautiously to the billabongs at sunset, drinking their water when the crocodiles are visible. The dingoes and kangaroos fade back into the savannah before nightfall.

This vast land was once the home of nomadic Aborigines, and though the entire Survivor locale is on private land and thus safe from trespassers from civilization, sometimes one or two of the few remaining Aboriginal wanderers will chance upon the location. Like the contestants will soon be doing, the Aborigines make their living through hunting, fishing, and gathering. Aboriginal legend says the area is haunted, and that the ghosts of a thousand scream some nights.

Tribal Council

Tribal Council is a long walk from the camps. Contestants will face a grueling trek each time, especially after the gravel banks give way to smooth cliffs of pink granite. The walk will be easier on hot days but terrible during rain, for the granite becomes slick as ice. As they get closer to Tribal Council, the river narrows and rapids begin to appear. The rapids bunch closer together, and soon the entire river is whitewater. The Tribal Council set is perched on the lip of Herbert Falls, some four hundred feet above a black pool. We have designed the forum for the *Survivor* decision using a combination of Stonehenge-like rock structure and Aboriginal symbolism that flows with the surroundings.

Challenges

Survivor's Challenges are the make-or-break aspect of contestant living. They're kept a secret from the cast until the day comes to film each new Challenge. Obviously, nothing specific can be mentioned about the Challenges in this space. But as a nod to the public's heightened expectations for *Survivor II,* let's just say *Survivor's* Challenges production department has doubled its manpower since *Survivor I* and was given a mandate to design Challenges on an epic scale. Stay tuned…

A FEW OUTBACK SURVIVAL TIPS THE ABORIGINES HAVE KNOWN FOR CENTURIES, MOST OF WHICH THE CONTESTANTS WILL IGNORE AT THEIR PERIL

- The sun can cause a burn in just fifteen minutes.

- Never walk barefoot.

- Do not walk around or over fallen timber.

- Always look for tracks on paths and sandy riverbanks. This will identify dangerous animals (reptiles, pigs, etc.) in the area.

- Don't eat berries, seeds, fruits, flowers, or mushrooms.

- When collecting firewood, always use a stick to overturn wood before picking it up. Fallen timber is an ideal habitat for snakes, spiders, scorpions, and centipedes.

- Never confront wild animals. If threatened, they will attack.

- Always check shoes before putting them on.

- When walking through the bush or along the riverbank, use a stick for spider webs. If you walk into a web, always find the spider. Make sure it is not on you.

- Do not stir food or water with sticks or twigs, as some contain toxins.

Deadly Hazards

Poisonous Snakes. The Aborigines worship a rainbow serpent named Kurrichalpongo. They believe that it created the world and its eggs hatched the mountains onto the earth and the trees into the ground.

The contestants will be on the lookout for the descendant of Kurrichalpongo at all times. Here's a short guide of what the various types of outback snakes look like, and how poisonous they are (on a scale of one to five, with five being the most poisonous).

Name: TAIPAN
Size: Six feet.
Appearance: Light to dark brown. Light-colored head.
On a scale of one to five (five being most poisonous),
how poisonous: 5.

Name: KING BROWN SNAKE
Size: Six feet.
Appearance: Dark red or brown. Pale on the underside.
How Poisonous: 4.

Name: WESTERN BROWN SNAKE
Size: Four to five feet.
Appearance: Narrow black head. Light brown body crossed by bands.
How Poisonous: 4.

Name: DEATH ADDER
Size: One foot.
Appearance: Triangular head, short tail. Gray or brown colors, crossed by bands.
How Poisonous: 4.

Name: COMMON BROWN SNAKE
Size: Four to five feet.
Appearance: Olive, gray, brown, or black, with a creamy belly.
How Poisonous: 4.

Name: BLACK WHIP SNAKE
Size: Three feet.
Appearance: Olive-brown or black.
How Poisonous: 1.

Spiders. It's a hard and scary thing to imagine, but spiders are more numerous and deadly than snakes in Australia. Contestants will be wise to give every spider web—there are plenty, both in the trees and on the ground—a wide berth. Most spiders are venomous and masters of disguise.

THE HUNTSMAN SPIDER: Lives under loose bark. Huntsman spider bites usually result in prolonged pain, inflammation, headache, vomiting, and irregular pulse. An ice pack may relieve some of the pain.

THE FUNNEL SPIDER: Lives underground. Bite is usually fatal.

REDBACK: Glossy black with a red streak down its back. A bite can cause paralysis, sweating, and tremors.

Freshies. Because the contestants will coexist in close proximity to freshwater crocodiles, it is expected they will be a key topic of discussion around the *Survivor* campfires. Though they're tough animals, the freshie is only dangerous when provoked.

A few facts: The freshie is a reptile. Its skin is scaly and, like all crocodiles, it is cold-blooded. The sharp claws are necessary for catching prey (crustaceans, spiders, fish, insects).

Running on the riverbank, the freshie moves at almost twenty miles an hour. An interesting feature is the smoothness of its long snout.

On the whole, contestants have nothing to fear from freshies.

Other Hazards. The end of the rainy season means mosquitoes will be less abundant. However, the black flies are infinitely more determined. They swarm about people, making it impossible to sit still without a swarm covering one's head, back, and arms. Their presence will be a constant annoyance.

Another fun flying thing is wasps. Contestants can expect a few stings.

Of course, neither flies nor wasps are a threat to life. But added to the constant danger of poisonous spiders, scorpions, and snakes, flies and wasps will render the outback a miserable place. Contestants will be hard-pressed to find a spot without some flying or slithering annoyance.

Food

The Protected List. This is a touchy subject. The outback is loaded with edible animals. Unlike Pulau Tiga (only in existence since an earthquake thrust it above sea level a hundred years ago), the outback has been home to mammals, reptiles, and snakes for ages. The Aborigine hunted them, learning which were edible and which were not. There had never been a lack of food in that great expanse, though it should be noted that outback critters are pretty sharp. They're renowned for keeping a low profile. At the first sign of a disturbance, outback animals disappear. Some say they'll run a mile to escape the slightest threat.

So can they be caught and killed? Sure. But not in this game. It's not allowed. Nobody's permitted to kill a kangaroo, wallaby, or wombat. Other protected outback animals include:

DINGO: This cunning hunter is similar to the American coyote. His main diet is birds and mammals. They sometimes hunt in packs and will then go after livestock, feral pigs, and kangaroos. The dingo will attack people.

EASTERN GRAY KANGAROO: The only kangaroo species living in the Herbert River area.

ECHIDNA: This cousin of the porcupine has a pointy snout and spiny quills. An extremely long tongue allows it to catch ants and termites. They use their sharp claws for digging into arboreal termite mounds.

COMMON WALLAROO: Halfway in size between the kangaroo and wallaby. Call it a demi-roo. This quiet animal thumps its foot to warn other wallaroos of danger. When an-noyed, however, they hiss and cough.

FLYING FOX: A bat, really. Their preferred food is eucalyptus blossoms and bush fruit. This means they actually function as an out-back version of bees, pollinating as they flit from plant to plant.

EMU: This wingless, hairy bird—no feath-ers—is the second largest bird in the world after ostriches. Their massive feet have three claws. The males make a distinctive grunting noise.

BRUSH TAIL POSSUM: Something of a varmint, the possum (like its American cousin) raids civilization for food.

SUGAR GLIDER: An Australian flying squirrel. Launching from high in a eucalyptus, it can travel almost one hundred yards.

And last, the most outrageous outback animal of all, the GOANNA. This lizard likes to build an extensive burrow system, but will gladly take refuge in a tree if a burrow can't be found. Goanna grow to six feet long, and move slowly on four feet. However, they can also rise up onto two feet and run very quickly. Sounds like something out of *Jurassic Park.*

A wondrous aspect of the outback is how visible these animals are. Spend a week along the Herbert and you'll catch a glimpse of them all.

The Unprotected Intruders. The contestants can, however, eat feral pigs. Brought to Australia by settlers a century ago, these non-indigenous porkers are the outback's version of rats, ubiquitous and annoying. They tend to be black or dirty white (or spotted). They'll charge if provoked. They have no manners and are unlikely to be domesticated. Food will have to be kept in trees or some other high place so the pigs don't get it. Given the chance, they'll nose around in a campsite until they find and eat every last edible product. They have excellent senses of hearing and smell, but poor eyesight.

Fish. Contestants will be able to catch fish (taking care not to annoy the freshies). The black bream is a bottom fish, living near snags, rocks, and weeds. Fins and spikes on either side of the gills make this footlong fish tough to grab. Better get the gaff.

The catfish is a cousin of American catfish. Another bottom feeder, the Australian cat features three sharp main fins that make picking it up dangerous.

Freshwater prawns and yabbys (crayfish) are abundant in billabongs and under rocks. The preferred way to catch them is by dangling meat into their habitat. Once they grab the bait, it's as simple as sweeping them up onto the bank.

Freshwater mussels. Though they can't be eaten raw (boiling is best) the freshwater mussel is quick, abundant food.

Plants. Edible wild berries will be in abundance. So will poisonous plants. It's up to the contestants to learn which berries and plants they can eat. On the edible list: wild tomatoes, cluster figs, rock figs, sand-piper figs (lots of figs!), water lily flowers (the stalk tastes like celery), emu berries, wild grapes, and native gooseberry are available and edible.

The bloodwood tree, a common gum tree, produces a sweet nectar. This can be dunked in a mug of water to produce a sweet, nutritious drink.

For an even fruitier taste, the she-oak bears green oak apples that can be chewed as a thirst quencher. The fruits have an extremely acidic taste.

If anyone catches the flu, the remedy is chewing or sucking on the bark of a paperbark tree.

Plants contestants will want to avoid include quinine (also known as bush orange), which causes sterility, and heart leaf, a member of the rho-dodendron family, which can kill after the ingestion of just one or two leaves. This bush is about five feet tall, with a blood-red flower.

The white cedar tree has an appetizing-looking fruit, but it's actually poisonous, causing death in children and livestock. The flowers are lilac and purple. Finally, lantana can cause severe diarrhea. In most environ-ments that wouldn't be a problem, but the dehydration of living in a desert environment means vital fluids are hard to come by. Diarrhea drains fluids from the body (also decreasing the individual's potassium level and causing weakness).

Mushrooms. All outback mushrooms and fungi contain toxins. They are all inedible.

A Word about Birds. Australia's birds are loud and colorful—much like Australia's human population. Contestants will set their body clocks by the birds. They're neither food source nor predator, but it's worth a second to mention the most common.

KOOKABURRA: Known for its distinc-tive laugh. It nests in a hollow tree or tun-nels into arboreal termite mounds. The kookaburra wakes up at dawn, then wakes up the rest of the world. Its colors are whitish-brown with a slight coloring of blue on the wing.

SULPHUR CRESTED COCKATOO: Think of Baretta. White bird, yellow crown, long white tail.

BLACK COCKATOO: A spectacular bird. Very large. Black with white tail feath-

ers. Aborigines believe that the Black Cockatoo is an omen of rain.

RAINBOW LORIKEET: A parrot. Lives in eucalyptus trees and feeds on nectar.

WHITE BREASTED SEA EAGLE: Australia's largest sea eagle. Also found inland where food sources are plentiful. Quite common along the Herbert.

WEDGE TAILED EAGLE: Australia's largest eagle. Preys on small mammals, including small kangaroos, sheep, and calves.

THE WHITE-NECKED HERON: A common water bird along the Herbert.

Water. Artesian wells are abundant in the outback. If they can find one, the contestants can either drink this water or, more likely, drink from the waters of the Herbert River. The latter isn't so simple, because of the potential for giardia from animals located far upstream.

Contestants can purify water by straining river water through charcoal and a sock. Though the water will be free of impurities, it will also taste like last night's campfire. A much easier—though time-consuming—process is boiling. Once they make fire, the contestants will get in the habit of boiling all water before drinking or eating. This means not just obtaining water from the river, but stoking the fire to keep it boiling.

Shelter

Contestants will need to build a home. Rain and heat will both be a problem, so the design should allow for adequate ventilation and a watertight roof. Also, the platform should be high off the ground to discourage snakes, spiders, scorpions, and other things that slither.

Contestants will find plenty of eucalyptus wood, leaves, and branches to serve as prime building material. Bark and thick range grass will plug any leaks.

Range Fires. The outback is deadly tinder during the Dry. Dead grass, fallen twigs and leaves, and hot temperatures combined with roaring winds make it a perfect fire zone. So it's no surprise that brushfires are numerous. It's Australia's policy to let them burn as a means of regenerating the soil. Contestants (and crew) will have to be wary of fires. A wind shift can turn a harmless, distant burn into a life-threatening situation in mere moments.

Choose Your Weapon. Contestants will take a cue from the Aborigines when it comes to weapons for catching food. Spears, for instance, will be handy for capturing feral pigs. The Aboriginal fish trap is an elaborate contrivance. Should the contestants be able to master its use they'll find it exceptional. Fish swim in, but can't swim out.

Climate. The contestants of *Survivor* will become intimately acquainted with northern Australia's temperature fluctuations. The dry season is slowly coming to an end as filming begins, but still temperatures skyrocket. The temperature on location will regularly be over 100°. The shade offers little relief, for it's a windless heat, resting atop an individual like an unwanted burden. It's worth noting that the outback's legendary flies and mosquitoes are especially prosperous in the hot months. The wet season, which slowly follows the dry, will arrive about midway through filming and account for almost all the one hundred inches of rainfall visited on the region annually. When it falls, the rain is torrential. River levels rise from sedate and shallow to roaring. Herbert Falls, the Tribal Council location and epicenter of island life, will be at full strength. The sight of whitewater pouring over this slick black rock cliff will be something few who witness it will ever forget. Choosing where they place their camps is pivotal, for what one day is a dry creek bed tomorrow can be a raging river.

Monsoons will also be likely during the contestants' time in the outback. Hot air mingling with cool ocean air will bring about that mixture of high pressure and low pressure systems that funnels air from the jet stream—four to six miles high—down to earth. Monsoons bring rain, extreme wind, and destruction. Just what the contestants need to enhance their *Survivor* experience.

Wildlife Survival Tips

For the most part, the critters of Australia are reclusive. They're famous for scampering a mile at the sound of people. Australia's infamous poisonous snakes, for instance, are passive, only attacking when provoked. However, accidents do happen. The foolish swimmer paddles into a freshie billabong, the unsuspecting hiker drops his rucksack on top of a coiled brown snake. This is life in the outback. It sounds foolish, but these mistakes happen every day. So what to do?

Crocodile attack. Stories of saltwater crocodiles (modern day dinosaurs) swimming up freshwater aren't just legend. These things happen all the time. Lucky for the contestants, to make it above Herbert Falls, the salties would have to be very ambitious, because it's a long way to climb. They'd also have to be physically capable of clambering up hundreds of feet of waterfall, which they are not. What the contestants will encounter in their area above the falls are freshies—freshwater crocodiles. These grow to be up to six feet long. And while that's small compared to a twenty-foot saltie, that's still a lot of reptile.

Obviously, the easiest preventive measure is staying out of the rivers and billabongs where freshies hide. Night is the worst time. In the highly unlikely event that the normally shy freshie attacks, the victim should shove his fist into the crocodile's mouth. There's a valve deep in the throat that prevents water from entering the airway. By forcing this valve open—and holding it open—water will enter the throat and the crocodile will begin to drown. Then the victim can escape. Good luck with that advice—I would probably die of a heart attack first.

OPPOSITE: Rodger and Nick

It's worth noting that freshies are naturally shy. They are not aggressive toward humans. However, stepping on a freshie, or disturbing a female guarding her nest, is a sure ticket to pain.

Snakebite and Spider Bite. Australian snakes are not predatory toward humans. Stay away from them and they'll stay away from you. The Taipan snake is a notable exception. As for spiders, they're even more lethal and common than snakes. Again, anti-venins are usually available.

Scorpion bites are painful but not

Herbert Falls

deadly, though they should be treated just as seriously as snakes or spiders.

Australian hospitals have the best anti-venins in the world, and there are antivenins available for every snakebite. It's just a matter of staying calm and following the proper procedures. It's important not to cut or wash the bite in any way. Also, avoid tourniquets or sucking. These techniques for treating snakebite are long discredited.

Tightly apply a bandage around the limb and on the bitten area.

Keep the limb and victim as still as possible. Bind some type of splint to the limb.

Bring transport to the victim if possible.

Leave the bandage and splint on until medical care is reached.

The *Survivor* crew suffered three snakebites before production began. Two were from tiger snakes, the other from a brown (who, thankfully, didn't inject his deadly venom). Fast medical action saved the day. After bouts of severe vomiting and nausea the injured crew members lived to tell the story.

The Crew

*S*urvivor: *The Australian Outback* has a bigger crew than the first edition. The roster is over twice as large and far more international, split almost evenly between Americans and Australians. This combination of manners and attitudes and manner of dress brings a surreal *Mad Max* quality to the proceedings. Most of the Americans worked on *Survivor I*, and have easily become the best in the business at producing full-tilt dramality. Their presence makes *Survivor II* one very solid production indeed. Their familiarity with each other also makes for a tremendous feeling of esprit de corps.

The Australian film industry is growing rapidly, and in many ways rivals the United States'. While the American crew hail from a background of both feature film and television, the Aussie crew members have focused more on features. Before *Survivor,* many had worked on *The Thin Red Line, Mission: Impossible 2,* and *Star Wars,* all of which shot at least part of their scripts in Australia. *Survivor,* having a crew of over two hundred and shooting on a remote set for forty-two days straight with an epic scale of production, much more closely resembles a film than TV.

Despite the close-knit feel of this eclectic bunch, *Survivor's* success means a greater focus on keeping The Secret the second time around. For security issues, only the host, producers, and camera crews are allowed to enter Tribal camps. Only "need to know" personnel are permitted to watch Tribal Council or the Challenges. Only a tiny hub of personnel know how the game is progressing. With such a large crew, the fewer that know what's going on, the less the chance of The Secret slipping out.

The crew compound is roughly four miles from the contestants. The crew lives in tents, with every crew member getting one to himself. A small complex of temporary trailers forms the suite of meeting rooms, offices, editing bays, and other production-necessary facilities. Crew all have access to Internet facilities and phones. It's fair to say the *Survivor II* location's boomtown feel is remarkably similar to the mining towns that sprung up overnight during the Aussie Gold Rush. And like the mining towns, the *Survivor II* location will disappear just as quickly as it came to life. A week after production wraps it will be so quiet and restored that the kangaroos will have forgotten we were here.

While production designer Kelly van Patter is responsible for the look and feel of the Tribal Council and all Challenges, the crew compound owes its look to unit manager Dick Beckett. He's in charge of all logistics, catering, and transportation. An ex-hippie in his forties and a living legend in film industry logistics, Beckett has been on more films than he can remember. Before production, he took one look at the quiet grove of eucalyptus trees destined for the crew compound and knew exactly what to do. Almost overnight he transformed the quiet grove into Survivortown. The big joke is that Dick owns every gas can, tent, generator, dish, and even light bulb in Australia—then rents it all to *Survivor.* Everything seems to have DB UNIT stenciled on it. One crew member joked that only the compound's wine bottles lacked the distinctive stamp. By the next morning Dick had rectified the problem. Every wine bottle in camp bore the DB UNIT logo.

Because the crew compound is so far from the contestants, transportation to and from the Tribal Council and contestant camps will be done by four-wheel drive. Also, the crew will have access to mountain bikes as a backup form of transport.

The crew will work upward of eighty hours a week, but that still leaves a lot of downtime. After a day of working, crew members will repair to The 42 Day Bar, a sprawling rustic pub. Beer, loud music, and dancing will be the order of the day.

Meet the Contestants

They are a cross section of American society. They are men and women, successful and struggling, married and single, of various ethnic backgrounds. Whether their motivation is money or empowerment or fame, all are adventure-seekers and prone to action, heeding an inner voice telling them they had what it took to compete on *Survivor*, despite the fact that friends and neighbors and coworkers laughed at the long odds.

Meet the sixteen new contestants for *Survivor: The Australian Outback*. Soon they will become the members of the Kucha and Ogakor tribes.

The interview process revealed that all are savvy about how to play the game. Unlike their predecessors, with their gentle naïveté and peaceful aversion to playing a game of alliances and subterfuge, the new corps know it will take a hard swallow of realpolitik to fly home as winner of a million dollars. As the game goes on, perhaps their will to triumph will soften as it butts hard against morality and childhood lessons about fair play. Or maybe not. The only thing for sure is that they will spend forty-two solid days in the outback.

That's right, forty-two. While the first *Survivor* was thirty-nine days and thirteen episodes long, *Survivor: The Australian Outback* will be just a tad longer, with a forty-two-day contest resulting in fourteen episodes. The drama moved quickly at the end last time, perhaps too quickly. It will be nice to savor the extra time with the contestants.

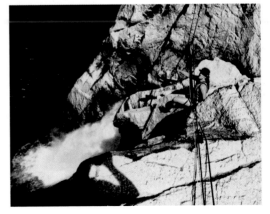

In addition to knowledge of The Game, are there pronounced differences in this new bunch? Sure. They're a little younger, a little more diverse, a little more prone to confrontation. They talk a little bit more about the money. They adopt a more callous air. They seem a little more sure that they know exactly how to win the game.

None of that matters. The game that began back in the summer of 2000 with forty-nine thousand prospective competitors battling for sixteen choice spots will end, as always, with just one winner. In the end, only one will be the Survivor.

KUCHA

Rodger

Debb

Jeff

Nick

Name: RODGER   *Age*: 53
Hometown: Crittenden, Kentucky
Marital status: Married
Profession: Teacher, Farmer
Quote: "I have got a good family life
with good family members and a nice
place to live...food on the table,
so what else is there, really?"

Name: DEBB   *Age*: 45
Hometown: Milan, New Hampshire
Marital status: Widowed
Profession: Corrections officer
Quote: "I've never done anything
in my life I have felt so strongly about."

Name: JEFF   *Age*: 34
Hometown: Greensboro, North Carolina
Marital status: Single
Profession: Internet project manager
Quote: "I'm winning the money, if it
means being ruthless or if it means
lying, so what...I am ready to be
there forty-two days, I'm ready to go!"

Name: NICK   *Age*: 23
Hometown: Steilacoom, Washington
Marital status: Single
Profession: Student, U.S. Army officer
Quote: "I don't want to be a leader.
Toning down my natural competitive
edge will be my toughest part."

TRIBE

Kimmi

Alicia

Elisabeth

Michael

Name: ELISABETH   *Age*: 23
Hometown: Newton, Massachusetts
Marital status: Single
Profession: Footwear designer
Quote: "My will cannot be taken
away from me; it is not equipment
and it's not something I lose."

Name: MICHAEL   *Age*: 38
Hometown: White Lake, Michigan
Marital status: Married
Profession: President of a software
publishing and distribution company
Quote: "I was told through
extensive psychological testing
that I was a control person."

Name: KIMMI   *Age*: 28
Hometown: Ronkonkoma, New York
Marital status: Single
Profession: Bartender
Quote: "Everybody goes to the Hamptons
to party and I'm the one who helps
them have a good time."

Name: ALICIA   *Age*: 32
Hometown: New York, New York
Marital status: Single
Profession: Personal trainer
Quote: "I am definitely going to have an
advantage over someone who comes
from a small rural town who isn't used
to dealing with the pressure of a lot
of people, personalities, and emotions."

OGAKOR

Amber

Keith

Colby

Kel

Name: AMBER   *Age*: 22
Hometown: Beaver, Pennsylvania
Marital status: Single
Profession: Administrative assistant
Quote: "I'm not going to come out
being blatantly mean but they are
going to know that I'm not the sweet
innocent girl that they can take advantage
of . . . I'm not going to let them."

Name: KEITH   *Age*: 40
Hometown: West Bloomfield, Michigan
Marital status: Divorced
Profession: Chef and restaurateur
Quote: "I dedicate this to my
kids, Josh and Alicia, and I'm just
gonna do the best I can do."

Name: COLBY   *Age*: 26
Hometown: Christoval, Texas
Marital status: Single
Profession: Custom auto designer
Quote: "My biggest weakness
is not being able to play the
Indian instead of the chief."

Name: KEL   *Age*: 32
Hometown: Fort Hood, Texas
Marital status: Single
Profession: U.S. Army intelligence officer
Quote: "I love adventure but
I also want the million dollars."

TRIBE

Jerri   Tina

Maralyn   Mitchell

Name: MARALYN   *Age*: 51
Hometown: Wakefield, Virginia
Marital status: Single
Profession: Police inspector, retired
Quote: "Perhaps this time there
will be a women's alliance,
a.k.a. 'a battle of the bitches.'"

Name: MITCHELL   *Age*: 23
Hometown: Vermillion, South Dakota
Marital status: Single
Profession: Singer, songwriter
Quote: "I want to keep the people
I want to be with; the cooler people,
that's who I want to be with."

Name: JERRI   *Age*: 30
Hometown: Los Angeles, California
Marital status: Single
Profession: Struggling actress
Quote: "I'm not the type of person
that likes to step on other people
or hurt other people's feelings,
but it is a game."

Name: TINA   *Age*: 40
Hometown: Knoxville, Tennessee
Marital status: Married
Profession: Nurse
Quote: "You are gonna have a party
as soon as you get rid of all the
mean, hateful, nasty people."

Casting

All of the *Survivor* contestants were put through an intensive casting process, including medical evaluations, interviews, and answering an extensive questionnaire. The comments of the casting director and psychologist Dr. Richard Levak and Q&As that follow give terrific insight into the contestants' motivations and their chances.

Kucha Tribe

RODGER FIFTY-THREE YEARS OLD/TEACHER, FARMER

Casting Director: "Southern gentleman with old-school values and charm; strong work ethic. Doing it for the over-fifty folks...will try to maintain order and discipline within his tribe until merger...then he'll watch the others spontaneously combust in a meltdown of conflict and hope they respect his levelheaded approach."

Psychologist: "Rodger could contribute a lot of practical skills; will get into difficulties with the huge range of diversity and strong women; not used to deferring to anyone younger or female."

What skills do you bring that would make you a useful member of the group?

I am a leader, inventive, hard working, physically fit, and most important, I can adapt to different situations and to different people. I will be the final Survivor.

What are your primary and secondary motivations for being on the show?

I always wondered how I would perform under these conditions to see if I have the "right stuff." To prove that a person over fifty can be the final Survivor.

Why would you be the final Survivor?

I am in very good health. I bike, walk, weight lift regularly. I am familiar with the outdoors. Heat does not bother me. I am industrious, energetic, inventive, and, even more important, I can relate to people of different ages, sexes, and beliefs. They would hate to vote me off.

JEFF THIRTY-FOUR YEARS OLD/INTERNET PROJECT MANAGER

Casting Director: "Hot, outspoken, opinionated, cocky, funny, not afraid to speak his mind; describes himself as aggressive, unpredictable, and strategic. Very calculating, analyzing and studying the competition from the moment he got on the plane; plans to lie low and evaluate; will have fun being manipulative and will probably instigate conflicts that he will then not participate in—he wants the money."

Psychologist: "Could win; is bright, has self-discipline, but it can break down under stress; a risk-taker who questions the rules; would get defensive in the face of criticism; has some underlying anger because he's had to struggle for everything in his life; may get sidetracked from goal of winning by getting caught up in showing up people who push his buttons."

What skills do you bring that would make you a useful member of the group?

People management, leadership, approachability, creativity, athleticism (run, climb, swim, etc.), competitiveness, iron will, agility, flexibility, positive attitude, sense of humor, conflict resolution, teaming, independence, dedication, loyalty, passion, survival instincts, resilience, common sense, and a willingness to try anything twice.

What are your primary and secondary motivations for being on the show?

I'd love the money, but conquering the challenge would be primary—pushing myself to achieve something I'm determined to do and experience it with an interesting mix of strangers. I've always thrown myself into fear and difficulty to grow, to become a stronger person. I'm in it for the person I'd be after it's over.

Why would you be the final Survivor?

I'd be the motivating member people would want on their team, as well as the formidable challenger (physically and mentally) a good competitor needs. I am an aggressive athlete, yet not a "super athlete." I don't think I'd be that much of a physical threat to anyone—at least until I needed to be. I consider my second home to be the woods of the Appalachian Mountains where I've lived, camped, fished, had sex, and wandered about aimlessly for years. My peace is found among its thick forests, placid lakes, amazing waterfalls and rapids—especially when it rains. I've hunted quite a bit and am very comfortable in the woods. I'd be focused and would search every moment, good and bad, for the positive it contained. I'd endure nature. I'm also a damn hard worker.

NICK TWENTY-THREE YEARS OLD/STUDENT, U.S. ARMY OFFICER

Casting Director: "Good looking, smart, cocky, ambitious, determined, and direct. Nick won't say a lot for a long time; will sit back and wait it out. Will be helpful and willing to participate for the greater good until it's time to flex his muscle and attempt to take control. Admits he's in it for money and fame."

Psychologist: "Would establish himself as a hardworking team member; likely to form alliances with older people and use their protection to strike out at young team members."

What skills do you bring that would make you a useful member of the group?
Intelligence, resourcefulness, and a keen sense of direction.

What are your primary and secondary motivations for being on the show?
I really could use a break from school. With a four-year commitment to the Army JAG Corps waiting for me after law school, my life seems too fragmented. Second motivation? Money and fame.

Why would you be the final Survivor?
You know, I read in the paper the other day all the crazy stuff people said they would do to be on the show and why they would win—whackos. I'd win because I'm a genuinely likeable guy with whom people seem to identify with. Plus, I'm in great condition and would work harder than anyone else.

DEBB FORTY-FIVE YEARS OLD/CORRECTIONS OFFICER

Casting Director: "Very opinionated, good talker; wants to win; honest, Middle America. Will try to organize the team to lead them to the merger with the advantage of more members; will try to form alliance with the less talkative people."

Psychologist: "Would become a stable core member of her team; would power struggle with any man who tried to assert his authority; could make it to the middle of the game because she's persistent and likable enough to be kept around."

What skills do you bring that would make you a useful member of the group?
I'm able to get along very well with others. I have powerful determination, common sense, and a great work ethic.

What are your primary and secondary motivations for being on the show?

Primary, I love living life. I want to try anything and be wild and crazy. Secondary, I am so curious to see the after-effects on my future life.

Why would you be the final Survivor?

I have always believed I could do anything. I'm certainly up for the challenge. Hey, it's the opportunity of a lifetime. I'm so excited I can't stand it!

ELISABETH   TWENTY-THREE YEARS OLD/FOOTWEAR DESIGNER

Casting Director: "Girl next door; cool look, slightly edgy, grounded, and full of life. Will be America's sweetheart. She's competitive, but she has the *'go team!'* spirit. Will make alliances with people you'd never expect her to hook up with."

Psychologist: "Would play same role as Colleen; would reflect on what's happening, but would get more outraged about what she perceived as unfairness and injustice, and strive to be positive, cheerful, and morally superior; would have a quicker temper if unfairly criticized or if people attempted to control her; would stand up for herself and the underdog; would vote based on moral beliefs rather than her likes or dislikes."

What skills do you bring that would make you a useful member of the group?
1) Creative problem solving
2) Athletic endurance/strength
3) Passion for a goal
4) The power to make a group of people work efficiently and devotedly together
5) High motivation instigation
6) A heart open to others

What are your primary and secondary motivations for being on the show?

Having the guts to go with my gut for once—proving to no one else but myself that I truly am armed to be a Survivor. The secondary motivation lies within my need to jumpstart my life.

Why would you be the final Survivor?

Because I have run two marathons. I am strong. I have overcome varied obstacles before. However, when it comes down to it, there are just those instances when you are granted certainty and though you cannot pinpoint a justified concrete explanation—you proceed with whole-hearted action.

ALICIA THIRTY-TWO YEARS OLD/PERSONAL TRAINER

Casting Director: "Pretty, sweet, great energy, physically fit; girls will like her and guys will want to sleep with her. Will remain cautious, yet competitive. Will act as the team player, but will not tolerate the weak members of her tribe."

Psychologist: "Will be fun, playful, and energetic; will confront people when she feels like it and will say what she wants; her hot button would be controlling or selfish men and then she would flare up; unfairness in the way men treat women could enrage her."

What skills do you bring that would make you a useful member of the group?
I would be a productive member of the group because of my creativity and attention to detail, given my artistic background, and a serious asset because of my physical strength and endurance.

What are your primary and secondary motivations for being on the show?
The first would be the challenge of putting my acquired life skills to the test. The second, one million dollars!

Why would you be the final Survivor?
I love a challenge and have a very competitive nature. When I put my mind to something I am persistent and focused on my own goal. However, even in situations of adversity I can keep my sense of humor and diplomacy helping me to perform well under pressure.

MICHAEL THIRTY-EIGHT YEARS OLD/PRESIDENT OF A SOFT-WARE PUBLISHING AND DISTRIBUTION COMPANY

Casting Director: "All-American funny dad; likes to talk; very entertaining; personality and looks. Believes his charm will win over his teammates; could put his foot in his mouth."

Psychologist: "He will be an entertainer who contributes a concrete skill of hunting to his team; he's not threatening to other men and likes women a lot; he's a contender for the finals because he's so good at selling himself to others."

What skills do you bring that would make you a useful member of the group?

I've hunted almost every animal, participate even today in many competitive sports and am in great shape. Great deal of common sense working with a group. Need very little sleep.

What are your primary and secondary motivations for being on the show?

The challenge is number one. I would have a blast, too. The money is third.

Why would you be the final Survivor?

I am a fighter to the finish. I've lived by the never-give-in philosophy for many years. I can survive in any condition. I sleep three to four hours per night. I am in excellent physical shape and work great with people.

KIMMI TWENTY-EIGHT YEARS OLD/BARTENDER

Casting Director: "Kimmi is sexy, playful; a real tease, very open and talkative. She will manipulate the guys in order to advance."

Psychologist: "She would be initially interesting and attractive to watch. However, Kimmi could eventually encounter trouble because of her tendency to say whatever comes to mind. Kimmi might not win, but will be fun to watch."

What skills do you bring that would make you a useful member of the group?

I'm resourceful, helpful. I work. I can lead or play along with the team.

What are your primary and secondary motivations for being on the show?

I want to challenge myself and prove to myself that I can accomplish whatever I put my mind to. I also want to laugh at everyone who said I'd never make it on. I guess a million bucks wouldn't hurt.

Why would you be the final Survivor?

I have the ability to look on the bright side of situations. I get along with most everyone. I listen to others but also speak my mind. I don't mind working hard, especially when at the end of the day I can sit back and be proud of seeing my accomplishments.

Ogakor Tribe

KEL THIRTY-TWO YEARS OLD/U.S. ARMY INTELLIGENCE OFFICER

Casting Director: "Knows it all, has an answer for everything; well-spoken, smart, opinionated, intimidating; Native American. Considers himself to be quite clever and feels he's got everybody sized up; will try to negotiate his way through the various personalities, but won't be able to keep his cool; wants the money."

Psychologist: "Underneath his control is an explosive and high-strung individual. Would try to prove himself through physical power, then attempt to gain control by winning respect. If not able to do that, he would become vulnerable to explosive episodes when people disagreed with him or challenged his authority."

What skills do you bring that would make you a useful member of the group?
I'm a soldier/officer. I've been trained to lead, kill, and to persevere under pressure. I am not a follower. As a leader I would motivate, plan, and lead from the front to get the job done.

What are your primary and secondary motivations for being on the show?
I want a million dollars so I can open up my own gym, pay off my school loans, and help my parents out during retirement. My second motive is that I want to see Australia, experience the wild outback. Also, I love challenges. I like going up against different challenges and winning. *Survivor* would be a challenge.

Why would you be the final Survivor?
I am mentally and physically tough. I am not afraid of any challenge. I would never quit. I would give it my all. I have strong analytical skills that I have developed as an intelligence officer. I would be constantly analyzing the situation and the other members on my team and deciding if there is a better way to attack. I love to win.

TINA FORTY YEARS OLD/NURSE

Casting Director: "Motorcycle-riding mom with southern accent; nurse for two paralyzed people. She's sweet. She's competitive. She may not have a complete handle on what she's in for; 'nice as apple pie' strategy."

Psychologist: "Would work hard to conform, to play the right role and fit in; could become rigid, falling back on religious principles if felt she wasn't doing well; tomboy who enjoys competing with men; may not win as she tends to be a follower of people with authority."

What skills do you bring that would make you a useful member of the group?

I can cook, hopefully, hunt. I'm a hard worker because I can't be idle. Joy, kindness, fun—all three making it easy to live with me. Athletics to help win the contest.

What are your primary and secondary motivations for being on the show?

Primary, the adventure and to fulfill my quest of living a life less ordinary.

Why would you be the final Survivor?

I have the physical ability to survive! I am a hard worker due to my energy level. I try to put myself in other people's shoes and treat people with love and kindness.

COLBY TWENTY-SIX YEARS OLD/CUSTOM AUTO DESIGNER

Casting Director: "Gen-X/cowboy: skydives, hunts, and rides bulls; great-looking guy's guy. He'll try to prove his worth through his abilities in the Challenges and try to be everybody's best friend; 'A true chief knows when to be an Indian'; will then try to weed out the strong once tribes merge (may try to form alliance with weaker members still left)."

Psychologist: "Would initially be valued for his brute strength and willingness to try and do anything; could have a blowup or two if he is pushed too far; may not make it to the end because he's insufficiently conniving."

What skills do you bring that would make you a useful member of the group?
1) Because of my profession, I am constructually inclined.
2) Great physical strength and stamina.
3) Focused intelligence.

What are your primary and secondary motivations for being on the show?
1) The incredible experience of being in Australia in this type of atmosphere and context. Wow!
2) This is the perfect timing in my life. A time of transition. A time of unsure future.
3) Challenge!

Why would you be the final Survivor?
Combined mental and physical strength. Adaptability with both people and surroundings. A true chief knows when to be an Indian.

JERRI THIRTY YEARS OLD/STRUGGLING ACTRESS

Casting Director: "Jerri loves camping, hiking, and being on TV; guys will love her and she will use it to her advantage. Jerri will flirt to form an alliance with the guys. However, at the same time, she will try to bond with the women one-on-one."

Psychologist: "Jerri would demonstrate her desert survival skills and surprise people by being competent, not just cute. She will try to use people, her looks, openness, and niceness to manipulate her way to the end without being suspected of being strategic."

What skills do you bring that would make you a useful member of the group?
My experience in the harsh desert environment, my athletic abilities, my leadership skills, my openness, my drive to win. I'm fun to be around, great sense of humor, communicate well, independent, yet great team player. Thoughtful, don't allow anyone to push me around. Good listener, diplomatic in my expression of ideas, intelligent, resourceful.

What are your primary and secondary motivations for being on the show?
Primary, for the adventure and opportunity to push myself beyond any survival situation I've been in before. Secondary, the million bucks!

Why would you be the final Survivor?

My desert survival skills are well honed. I can acclimate to any given situation with openness and excitement, and I want this more than anything in the world.

KEITH   FORTY YEARS OLD/CHEF AND RESTAURATEUR

Casting Director: "A flirtatious schmoozer; divorced with two kids. He hopes that the others will respect his ability to provide (à la Rich Hatch); admits we'll likely see a transformation in his personality as days go by and people are voted off; will likely start out as the fun loving 'yes man,' happy to be of service to others. Wants the money."

Psychologist: "Would be cleverly manipulative, hanging back at first and watching for opportunities; would try to please people and win them over through nurturing them and cooking for them; has an explosive edge when crossed or irritated."

What skills do you bring that would make you a useful member of the group?

I can catch, kill, and create! As you know by now, I'm a chef! You can plunk me down almost anywhere and I can create a gourmet dining adventure! I have found that most people love to eat and drink well, so, why do you think they ask you what you want for your *final* meal?! I will also be the group's chef and start making outback delectables upon arrival. I have also been known to be a good leader. I'm also a bit of a prankster, so I'd keep people laughing. I thrive on stress-related situations. I can handle the unpredictable.

What are your primary and secondary motivations for being on the show?

Primary, the money. A million dollars would go a long way to ensuring a college education for my children—something I always wanted to do, but couldn't afford it. Secondary, I have adventure in my blood and this is the ultimate adventure!

Why would you be the final Survivor?

As a divorced Dad who turned forty this year, I feel like this would be the ultimate test for a guy who's never quite fit in. I know I will contribute solid survival skills and life skills to be one of the last survivors in Australia.

AMBER TWENTY-TWO YEARS OLD/ADMINISTRATIVE ASSISTANT

Casting Director: "Tomboy with a beautiful face and wild adventurous side; is a player. She will try to use her 'aw, shucks' looks and demeanor to come across as non-threatening. Before anyone realizes it, she may be in the final four."

Psychologist: "Not likely to last long. Her sweetness, youth, health, and good nature may not carry her all the way."

What skills do you bring that would make you a useful member of the group?
    An excellent swimmer, tree climber, fast runner, and I enjoy handling snakes.

What are your primary and secondary motivations for being on the show?
    Need a change, excitement, and kangaroos (primary). Lack of one million dollars (secondary).

Why would you be the final Survivor?
    Because the host visited me in a dream and told me I'd be the final Survivor.

MITCHELL TWENTY-THREE YEARS OLD/SINGER, SONGWRITER

Casting Director: "Defines charismatic; seven feet tall, funny and fun. 'Guys just wanna have fun.' His only strategy is to have a good time and make people laugh."

Psychologist: "Mitchell would delight his teammates with his humor; would work hard and be friendly to all but may not have the stamina emotionally or physically to pass initial stages; women will mother him. He will use his resources well enough to get through."

What skills do you bring that would make you a useful member of the group?
    Plain and simple, I would supply light-hearted humor and maintain a smile through thick and thin to cheer up even the grumpiest of grumpies.

What are your primary and secondary motivations for being on the show?
    Primary is easy: I'm always up for a good adventure! Secondary, it's on my "List of Things to Do Before I Die." So you either let me on the show or I'll have to make up a show called *Survival* and con my friends into doing it.

Why would you be the final Survivor?

Because I have the essential traits of the Final Survivor. You must be friendly, a leader, adventurous, yet work hard. You must have respect for, and think of, the others in order to get their respect in return. You must be positive and optimistic and above all else, be a young and hip hussy, which I am!

MARALYN   FIFTY-ONE YEARS OLD/POLICE INSPECTOR, RETIRED

Casting Director: "Brash, rough around the edges; wants to go to challenge herself and quit smoking; a real character. She will not be able to tolerate the weak and will try to vote them off, even though she may lose sight of the bigger picture; she wants a woman to win, so she may try to form an alliance with some of the women (but not at the expense of having to tolerate the annoying, weak-minded ones)."

Psychologist: "Would play her regular self-deprecating role with caustic humor until she found a better role to help her win; would look to someone to lead her. She will add spice and color."

What skills do you bring that would make you a useful member of the group?

Planning, organizational skills, leadership, creativity, resourcefulness, people skills, fitness, adaptability.

What are your primary and secondary motivations for being on the show?

To experience the challenge of a lifetime and to quit smoking.

Why would you be the final Survivor?

Based on my personal makeup, background, experience, and maturity, there's a good chance.

The Host: Jeff Probst

In addition to *Survivor,* Probst has helmed a variety of television shows. He was one of the original on-air talents for the FX network, hosting several shows and logging thousands of hours of live television. He was also one of the original correspondents for the syndicated entertainment news show *Access Hollywood.* He is currently the host of VH1's *Rock & Roll Jeopardy.* Probst recently wrote and directed his first feature film, *Finder's Fee.*

During the filming of the first *Survivor* series in Borneo, Probst was stung by a jellyfish in his nether regions. In Australia, Probst suffered a shock from an electric fence to his nether regions. For the next *Survivor,* Probst will be wearing a protective cup.

Chapter Five

Strategy

What's the Best Strategy for Playing *Survivor*?

Be it on the show or in the corporate world, there is no best strategy. Like any complex game, *Survivor* has myriad strategies. There is no right or wrong way to behave, there are merely paths to ultimate survival. For every contestant, this path will be different. The game's only guarantee is that putting up a deceptive facade is useless—*Survivor* is like a truth serum, ferreting out the strengths and weaknesses of an individual's personality. Sooner or later every contestant reveals his or her true self, no matter how hard he or she tries to disguise it.

Perhaps because the word "survival" is so often equated with outdoor adventure, it's hard for many to think of it in a social sense. They bridle when psychology is introduced, especially the armchair psychology of casual observers, as if only trained professionals are allowed to pass judgment on morals and motivations. In a perfect world, that would be the case. But the real world isn't perfect; people judge each other every day. The *Survivor* world is no different. It's important to understand that psychology is the very essence of the game. The player unwilling to understand the psychology guiding his opponents is the player destined for failure. Psychology is the bedrock of success in life and in *Survivor*.

The term Machiavellian is also used to describe *Survivor*, implying that victory can only be achieved through some sort of cunning or willingness to sacrifice friendship for the sake of victory. In many ways, this is correct. But it's very possible for a contestant to win the competition without such actions. It's all in how a contestant chooses to play the game.

During the first *Survivor*, the majority of the contestants came to the island without a plan. They would simply hang out, pull their weight (or not), act really friendly to everyone to avoid getting voted off, then fly home with a check for a million dollars. Only Richard Hatch strategized beforehand, realizing that the careful building of alliances with his fellow contestants would guarantee island longevity. Using a strategy that has now become legendary (and made Richard synonymous with Machiavellian), Richard crafted the Tagi Alliance. This close-knit core group of four slowly voted everyone else off the island. Richard, to the surprise of many, won *Survivor.*

Doubtless, this means that the contestants on *Survivor: The Australian Outback* will begin building alliances from Day One. Instead of being open and honest, as in the early days of *Survivor: Borneo,* the men and women of *Survivor: The Australian Outback* will be crafty, shielding their true personalities, pretending to be stronger or smarter or weaker or dumber than they really are. They will secretly meet like minds and build relationships. Others will be added to the alliance if it becomes strong, and fellow contestants will be carefully selected for expulsion. Maybe the ringleader of this alliance, à la Richard with his nude strolls along Tagi Beach, will even flaunt his or her security through some outrageous deed.

But, remember, the truth will out. Over the course of forty-two long days and nights of round-the-clock scrutiny by cameras, hunger, fatigue, heat, bugs, and the omnipresent suspicion of fellow contestants, everyone will crack. Their true personalities will reveal themselves. The personas displayed to all the world will be perceived as lies, engendering animosity.

Or not.

See, that's the beauty of *Survivor.* What happened on the first version may happen again on the second, or it might not. All bets are off. In this manner, *Survivor* is very much like the corporate world it echoes. Just as there is no single strategy for success in the corporate world, no single strategy will work on *Survivor.* It's worth noting that a great portion of Richard's success was due to luck. He was almost voted off twice, his alliance was almost in the minority before the tribal merger, his outrageous behavior very nearly went too far. All those things that now look like the acts of a genius were also subject to the whims of fate. If not for Richard's good luck, Colleen or Rudy or Kelly or Sue might have taken home the million. You never know.

Survivor is social Darwinism. That's the key. The winning strategy is whichever combination of attributes and actions an individual is flexible enough to acquire and make to convince others not to vote him or her off as the game evolves.

Great Castaways through History
(and Their Strategies for Survival)

Robinson Crusoe

In August 1704, a troubled Spanish sailor named Alexander Selkirk (aka Robinson Crusoe) jumped ship as his vessel sailed from Mas a Terra Island after a supply stop. There were goats, trees, and plenty of fresh water, and Selkirk enjoyed a good life.

Survival Skills: Strength through Solitude. Mas a Terra was near the strategic island of Juan Fernandez, which was visited regularly by Spanish and British ships. Selkirk could have been rescued almost anytime, but chose to remain alone.

Rescued? Eventually. After four years and four months, Selkirk got tired of being alone. He allowed the *HMS Duke* to take him home. Since then, Mas a Terra has been renamed Robinson Crusoe Island.

Dead Man's Chest

Legend has it that at the turn of the eighteenth century legendary pirate Blackbeard faced a mutinous crew. Blackbeard took swift action. He deposited the thirty mutineers on a barren island. There was no edible vegetation. Save for rainfall, there was no fresh water. There was a neighboring island just four hundred yards away, but Blackbeard was confident none of the pirates knew how to swim.

Blackbeard sailed away, but left the stranded pirates two implements: a cask of rum and a cutlass. In parting, he told the sailors he would return in a month to pick up any survivors.

Survival Skills: Strength to control the cutlass. Self-control to stay away from that cask. A previously hidden knack for swimming great distances.

Rescued? Yes. A month later, Blackbeard returned. The rum was gone and fifteen of the pirates were dead. As the island's profile, from a distance, bore a striking resemblance to the chest of a man lying flat on his back, it was given the nickname "Dead Man's Chest."

Shackleton

Antarctic explorer Ernest Shackleton set sail from England on the *Endurance* in August 1914. His plan was a trek across Antarctica from the Weddell Sea to the Ross Sea via the South Pole. En route, the *Endurance* became trapped in the pack ice surrounding Antarctica. As the helpless men looked on, the ice crushed the ship into splinters, stranding Shackleton and his crew of twenty-seven on an ice floe, where they lived for six months until it broke apart. The group then set out in open boats for the South Shetland Islands. However, finding them unable to sustain life, Shackleton undertook a perilous eight-hundred-mile journey across the Southern Ocean with a group of five handpicked men.

Survival Skills: Uncommon determination, the ability to ignore anxiety, and a superhuman ability to endure a life without privacy aboard an ice floe.

Rescued? Amazingly, yes. Even after landing on South Georgia Island after sixteen days at sea, Shackleton and his men still required a nonstop thirty-six-hour hike over a mountain pass to reach the safety of a whaling station. By August 30, 1916, Shackleton had returned to the men left behind in the South Shetlands and delivered them all to safety.

Swiss Family Robinson

The Robinson family were a fictitious German family who spoke with a mixture of English and American accents. They came to life in 1960 as a movie from Walt Disney Studios. In the story, Father and Mother Robinson and their three sons, Fritz, Francis, and Ernst, flee Napoleon as he conquers Europe. They are looking for someplace to live in the South Seas when their ship is sunk by pirates. The ship's crew desert the sink-

ing vessel and perish. However, the Robinson Family remains on board. When their ship finally founders on the rocky shoreline of a tropical paradise, the Robinsons build an ingenious tree house home from artifacts of the wrecked vessel. A young woman is added to their ranks through a subsequent shipwreck. The Robinsons and the attractive young lady discover love, tigers, and pirates on the lush island.

Survival Skills: For Father and Mother, rock-solid parenting abilities. With two sons in the throes of puberty and only one available woman, tact is of the essence.

Fritz has an epic duel with a reticulated python that proves a coming-of-age metaphor. Though the girl doesn't see the battle, it's symbolically fitting when he then wins her hand.

Rescued? Mother and Father, still anxious about Napoleon, elect to remain behind when a British ship stumbles across the island and offers rescue. The same holds for Fritz and his new friend. Francis and Ernst return to civilization to find their own Edens.

Elisabeth

Mutiny on the Bounty

On April 28, 1789, having had enough of Captain William Bligh's fascination with his shipment of breadfruit (bound from Tahiti to the Caribbean for planting as a new foodstuff), Lieutenant Fletcher Christian leads a mutiny aboard the HMS *Bounty*. Bligh and eighteen loyal crew members are not killed, but set adrift in the ship's launch.

Knowing that the Royal Navy will hang him and the other mutineers if they ever catch up with them, Christian sails to Tahiti for refuge. However, Tahiti is a popular stopover for British vessels. Christian does not feel safe. He sails again, and finds Pitcairn Island. This speck in the South Pacific halfway between Australia and South America offers food, water, and other resources to maintain life. Christian sinks the *Bounty* and starts a new life.

Survival Strategies: Two things: First, act decisively, consequences be damned. Several of Christian's fellow mutineers didn't heed his advice to flee Tahiti. They were later caught and returned to England, where three of them were hanged.

Second, the Adam and Eve strategy. When Christian sailed from Tahiti, he brought along twelve Polynesian women but only six other men. No dummy, that Fletcher Christian.

Rescued? Nope. Their society was discovered in 1808, but Christian and his people were not prosecuted or extradited. Their new civilization remains today, with most of Pitcairn's current residents able to trace their ancestry to the *Bounty*. In 1957, its remains were found at the south end of Pitcairn.

Mutiny on the Bounty, Part II

Fletcher Christian is the better-known half of the *Bounty* history, but the better story belongs to Bligh. After Bligh and his loyal nineteen were set adrift, Bligh undertook an ambitious voyage toward safety in the open boat.

His situation could not have been worse. He was stranded in the world's largest body of water, the Pacific Ocean. His boat was overcrowded. The equatorial sun baked him and his supporters. Wind and waves tended to be either nonexistent or hellacious. There was little food and even less water. To top it all off, Bligh was a tyrant. While the men in the boat supported him, many did so out of fear of naval punishment. They must have wondered again and again why they would ever choose

Tina

an open boat over the prospect of a life in Tahiti, a locale notorious in the sailing community for being a sailor's sexual paradise. How many times, facing death and another long day in the sun, did Bligh have to set aside his domineering ways to raise rock-bottom morale?

Survival Skills: A lot of talent mixed with a bloodlust for revenge and will to live. Bligh had an awful personality, but he was a genius. His navigational skills, knowledge of wind and weather and currents, and sixth sense of how a boat should behave is what allowed him to climb through the ranks from able seaman to captain. The only other man to accomplish this feat was Captain Cook.

Rescued? Actually, they rescued themselves. Bligh guided the small boat thirty-seven hundred miles to Timor on the Malayan Archipelago. No one died en route. Bligh then successfully arranged passage back to England, where he testified at the court-martial of the apprehended mutineers. There was a mutiny on Bligh's next command, too. And while Bligh was exonerated by an Admiralty court, he was quietly relieved of command and shipped off to distant Australia to serve as governor.

The Passengers and Crew of the S.S. *Minnow*

These denizens of *Gilligan's Island* began their odyssey with a simple three-hour cruise. The starting locale is commonly considered to be Honolulu, but knowledgeable insiders know from the show's opening credits that the *Minnow's* last contact with land was clearly the rocky jetty marking the entry to the harbor of Newport Beach, California. After that, the weather stared getting rough. The tiny ship was tossed. If not for the courage of the fearless crew, the *Minnow* would be lost.

And it was.

Eventually, the ship ran aground on the shores of an uncharted desert isle. With Gilligan, the Skipper, too; the Millionaire (Thurston Howell III) and his wife (Lovey); the Movie Star (Ginger Grant); The Professor, and Mary Ann.

Under the guidance of the Professor, a man with a MacGyver-ish ability to build everything from radios to eyeglasses with a coconut shell and bat guano, the first castaways in CBS history built a small settlement. Their huts were made of palm fronds atop a bamboo frame. Everyone shared a hut with one other castaway (Skipper and Gilligan; Mary Ann and Ginger; Thurston Howell III and Lovey) with the exception of the Professor, whose hut also doubled as a laboratory. A communal eating area featured a picnic bench–style table. Mr. Howell owned a still, fabricated from bamboo and gourds.

Survival Skills: The *Minnow*'s castaways had survival strategies matching their personalities:

> Skipper—benevolence.
> Gilligan—dementia.
> Thurston Howell III—wealth, martinis.
> Lovey Howell—an endearing lack of spatial awareness.
> Professor—genius.
> Ginger—sex appeal, evening gowns.
> Mary Ann—coconut cream pie.

Amber

As a group, this unlikely assortment of individuals had several strategies for survival. They constantly engaged in building rafts, small planes, and other devices designed to get them "off the island" (a favorite term of these castaways). Occasionally, visitors would stumble onto the island and the castaways would try to convince these newcomers to help them get back to civilization. They engaged in a variety of schemes, charades, and swindles to encourage the visitors' assistance, but to no avail.

The most remarkable aspect of this group's time on their island was the esprit de corps. With the exception of the occasional flare of petty jealousy or selfishness, the *Minnow*'s castaways worked exceptionally well as a unit.

Rescued? In the TV movie sequel.

Contestants' *Survivor* Strategies

How are the sixteen new contestants planning to play the game?

Kucha Tribe

RODGER

Basically, Rodger wants to start off low-key. "I'm certainly not going in like B.B. and hollering at some of the kids because they are not working. For the kids that don't pull their load I'm going to put their name up on the camera."

After getting selected as a contestant for *Survivor,* Rodger said it was tough keeping it quiet in a school of 950 kids and teachers. He had

ABOVE: Rodger

OPPOSITE: Nick

to tell the principal and superintendent so they could grant him a leave of absence and he says they have been really great about it. Going into the competition, Rodger says his previous work at a bank judging people for loans will assist him in his perception of the other players. However, he also knows that *Survivor* is a game and the others know that, too. So, his usual easygoing type persona might not work that well. "Sometimes I'm a little critical of people who don't carry their load. If we are building a shelter that eight people are going to sleep in, it is my feeling that all eight people should help in the building of it...that's probably not the way it's going to be so I'll just keep my cool, do my share, and not overdo." He does not want to look too strong in that area, so if the rest of them go under a shady tree, he will be there right with them.

Overall, Rodger is pretty satisfied with his life before *Survivor.* "I'm pretty well satisfied with the way things are going now...I have got a good family life with good family members and a nice place to live... food on the table, so what else is there, really?"

Finally, the one thing his daughter says will hurt his chances in the game will be his old-fashioned ways. For example, his wife has to lay out his clothes for him in the morning because he cannot seem to match colors.

NICK

Nick's basic strategy is to use his likability while analyzing and thinking quickly. He plans on weeding out the weak early on but at the same time does not want to assume a leadership role. Nick admits that it will be hard for him, but he wants to downplay his intelligence. "I don't want to be a leader. Toning down my natural competitive edge will be my toughest part. Otherwise, people will get annoyed with me or think that I am trying to show them up." Nick believes that competitive people, though they may do well and help, will rub people the wrong way. If such competitors remain after the merge, he will let them win in order to make it look like they are showing up the rest.

Looking back on the first show, Nick definitely related in a lot of aspects to Gretchen because she was a well-rounded, nice person who did good things and was respected for it. Even though he did not relate to Greg's personality, Nick thought that Greg was great by not taking it all too seriously. However, he thought Greg, being as smart as he was, did not use his wit as best as he could in playing the game.

Nick is concerned about the way people view him. He wants to be seen as intelligent but does not want to be seen as a threat. He wants to portray an image of being open and nice. "I'm generally pretty likable, which is important. To do well on this show, you have to always be thinking right from the start. You must focus from day one on who you interact with, what you say, what you are doing, and what you are not doing. You have to be really conscious of how people view you and the image you are portraying."

He does not want to reprimand people if they are not getting the job done. He wants to find out what each person is good at so they find a niche. "I may hold my tongue if I think it is wise to hold my tongue." However, the bottom line for Nick is that he is there to win and every-

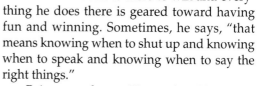

thing he does there is geared toward having fun and winning. Sometimes, he says, "that means knowing when to shut up and knowing when to speak and knowing when to say the right things."

Being a student at Harvard and being intelligent plays a big part in Nick's everyday life and will play heavily in the outback. "I'm a normal guy. People have opposite reactions when you say Harvard: either they are in awe, or they say, 'This guy is rich and snobby,' which is not the case."

Nick attributes his days in Harvard to

hard work rather than sheer intelligence. He says that in order for him to do well, he has to downplay his association with Harvard. Also, he wants people to know that after Harvard he is not just going to graduate, get a high-paying job, and be rich. "I'm gonna be doing public service in the military and then, if I can, continue in law in some government facility."

JEFF

Jeff says that he feels very prepared and he has worked all the angles. "I'm winning this money, I mean, I intend to win it. I'm not going there for vacation; I'm not going there to make friends; I don't care about any of these people. I'm voting them off one at a time; I'm winning the

money; if it means being ruthless or if it means lying, so what? I'm prepared to be there forty-two days, I'm ready to go!" He feels that alliances that will last will take a while to form. Jeff believes that alliances will try to form immediately, "as soon as our feet hit the ground." Jeff implies that he may fake alliances initially and then form a sub-alliance; he is willing to lie to win. "I'm going to be a very smart player in this game. I'm gonna be very flexible; I'm gonna be on my toes throughout the whole thing. Everybody is going to play very strategically, I feel. I cannot imagine choosing people who wouldn't form alliances."

Jeff has thought through his game plan very carefully. "I've played the pieces and the numbers together so I have many different scenarios in my mind of what could potentially happen and I have a couple of other things that I have thought through...being prepared for whatever happens, being able to watch other people. I'm very self-aware; I know how I'll react to certain situations, and I feel I can judge people and size character fairly quickly, just being on my toes and being able to employ the right strategy at the right time. I think it is what is needed in order to play. Anybody who walks in the door with a blanket strategy saying this is the way I'm gonna play this game and this is the way we are playing through the whole thing, put them in my tribe."

Upon reflection of last season, Jeff says that he related to Richard immediately. "On Day One, if somebody starts trying to trump up people and orchestrate people and orchestrate the group as a team dynamic, I will immediately know that that is someone I need to keep an eye on." Jeff believes that the new group of sixteen will enter this competition much smarter and much more prepared than the last group did. He says

that this is mainly because the new group now knows how the game is played, but also because they have seen the last sixteen on television and in magazines evaluate themselves and the way that they played the game. Jeff is prepared for anything. He insists that he is a hard worker and a responsible person, so if he is in the middle of a group that prefers not to go down that road and not have fun, then he says he will adapt and adjust to do what he needs to do.

Jeff wants to step outside of his everyday life and step into *Survivor*. "I'm playing a game. In my life, I am a certain person and the people who know me know and respect me because I tell the truth and I treat people kindly; I'm a motivator, very much a team person. *Survivor* gives me an opportunity to step outside of that and play this game that these people play everyday. I deal with politics every day and I hate it, it burns me up and wears me down; this gives me an opportunity to play it for a little while."

DEBB

The contestant from *Survivor* that Debb related to most was Gretchen. Unlike Gretchen, however, Debb would initiate an alliance to stay in the game. "My biggest overall strategy is to go and play it by ear, but I am not going to be stupid; I'm not gonna think it's a big old game because there is more at stake than just a game. If you are too strong, they are going to boot you out the door. If you are too weak, they are going to boot you out the door. It's going to be such a game of maneuvering and outwitting. The outwitting is going to be the big thing. I took a test at the prison to see how well I would do working in a block with inmates, and I scored the highest you can score at being able to bend to different personalities. That may be the key. I know that I can bend to different personalities; I don't have to like someone to work with them and get along

OPPOSITE: Mitchell and Amber

with them. I can get along with people pretty easily; I guess I'll have to watch my temper because I can get a little hot at times.

"You are going to have to learn to work with these people, whether you get along with them or don't get along with them, whether you like their ideas or you don't; somehow or other you are going to have to find a common ground to get along."

Debb feels she's a strong woman, experienced at dealing with men, who

has endured a great amount of hardship. These attributes make her a great survivor. "I was married for almost seventeen years. My husband was a police officer who was killed on duty. He was working on a case. Now I have a boyfriend but am not married. I work in a men's prison. I wanted a job where I could do what I love to do and that's order men around, lock them up if they do not behave; I cuff them and lug them. As a rule, the inmates respect me; they know that I'm there to do my job and treat them with respect.

"If I go up to a man and give him an order, he is 99 percent of the time going to do what I say. But if a guy goes up and gives an order in the same respectful tone of voice, they are gonna say, 'Go to hell, I'm not doing it.' It's just a thing with men. Men take directives better from women. At least in prison they do."

Debb adds that she is compassionate, which will help on *Survivor.* In prison, she says, "There are people who have lost their freedom for one reason or another. I go in and try to make their life bearable while they are losing their freedom. The inmates were laughing at me when I told them I filled out an application for *Survivor.* They said I was crazy and asked me how I would get along with those sixteen people. I looked at them and said, 'How do you think I get along with you?'"

I knew when I saw that application that I was going to be on that show. Everybody tells me that I'm one of a kind. I have inner strength and I never quit. People sometimes confuse me with cocky. I'm not cocky at all; I just don't quit because I believe in myself. I believe I can do something and I don't care if I fall down and I don't care how many times. I am going to get up and I will eventually succeed.

"I can work fine with people; I just don't like weak people who can't make decisions. If I'm with strong people, I'm gonna be fine with them, but you get me together with someone like Ramona—I know she was sick. But get up! Get up! This is a chance of a lifetime. Don't just sit there with your stomachache. Get up! Put me with the strong people and I'm fine; I just don't like losers. So much is going to depend on the dynamics that are happening and personalities and stuff. It's hard for me to sit in this chair and say what I'm gonna do; I'm gonna do everything I need to do to win. I'm not going there to take second place.

"In the past, I have not trusted myself when I should, so I'm just gonna go over there and play the game. I'm going to play it smart and I'm gonna have a blast doing it, because my first and foremost goal is to have a good time. This is an adventure of a lifetime."

ELISABETH

Elisabeth related to Rudy most of all the previous contestants. She liked his truthfulness and steadfastness. She also related to Colleen. However, she thought Rich was too serious from the very beginning. Her plan is to be true to herself, because she's not a good actor. She also has a big problem with dishonesty. "I was captivated by Rudy, drawn to him because there are so many people now who change their ways; I admired how steadfast he was and just how matter-of-fact. That was a lovable quality. If I were to have someone on my team, it would be someone like Rudy. The other was Colleen. I identified with her. She'd be someone in my environment that I'd love to hang out with and talk to." Regarding Rich, "You can't say he did anything wrong, he won."

As for her own strategy, Elisabeth plans to follow the road less traveled. "I'd like to give a little shake and do something a little different; have it kind of unfold a different way than the first one did. I think there are different ways to win and the first *Survivor* showed you one way, and I'd like to kind of shake it up a little bit and do it my way.

"My will cannot be taken away from me; it is not equipment and it's not something I lose. I don't feel the need to trick people, or to lead them to believe I'm one way when I'm not. Some people would disagree because they think that you need to be deceitful and conniving out there. I just know I can make it fun even when times are tough, because people will need that little kick. I've done some camping; I have to say I'm more prone to going to the city and do things more urban like that."

Despite her relative lack of experience, Elisabeth feels she's ready to play. "It's just been a gut feeling about *Survivor*. It encompassed everything I love; it has the physical challenges, which gets me fired up. It's a new place, which I'm so excited to see, and right from the beginning my gut told me I should do it, and whenever I go with that, it is right. It's something that captivated me to the point where I was seeing myself on it and I loved it. It's easy to be strong and say you are going to do something when you are not. Put in an element that's testing you physically and emotionally, and I think that's when you have to have that strength of will to keep yourself going. I know when someone is not on the right track and it hits me like a ton of bricks and I know. When someone is not loyal and is acting dishonest, I have no tolerance for it, because we have the ability to make a decision

and make a good one, and when someone doesn't, I just see them as weak and it really ticks me off.

"It's a fault of mine that I give someone my trust, pretty much my all, and I let them prove me wrong for the most part, and that's something I will have to watch, obviously, because people's motives will be a little fired and more directed this time. I can now walk into a room and just sense how people are."

ALICIA

Alicia admits to having a strong personality and wants to downplay that. "I have to be really careful about coming across too strong, because that is naturally what will happen. If I step back and try to be people's friends, which is easy for me to do, then I won't be threatening to them. I have to be careful, because my biggest concern is that I will actually be a big threat."

Her plan is to become friends with everybody instantly and Alicia is determined to win all the Challenges. "I would like to have a strong team in the beginning, try to win every Challenge, so that we can go into the merger with as many people on our team as possible and outnumber the other team. Hopefully, by then, alliances will be formed, because that's got to happen in order for people like myself, who are considered threats, to stay on."

Also, she plans to be strong from the beginning and will initiate alliances. "I'd like to be in a leadership position in the beginning. I definitely want to win all the Challenges, so then I don't have to worry about Tribal Council. But when the tribes merge, that's when strategy will be very, very important, because at that point it's not about team dynamics any more, it's about individuals." Alicia believes that if she is asked to join an alliance that is not worthwhile for her, she might have to consider it anyway because she does not want to give anyone a reason to vote her off.

Looking back on the first *Survivor*, Alicia related to Gretchen because she liked her levelheadedness. Alicia believes that Gretchen was stuck in a tribe with a lot of younger people and that she was out of her element as far as her age group was concerned. "However, she kept it together and assumed the leadership role right from the beginning." Alicia's own game plan is to not care what people's perceptions are of her, because the people who really know her in life know what she is about. She knows that *Survivor* is a game and that she is playing for a million dollars that she would rather not lose because she worried about what people thought.

Alicia is a personal trainer whose typical clients are New York "ladies who lunch." She has both gym and in-home clients. Alicia believes her interaction with people throughout her workday will help her with her relationships in the outback. "You train people hour to hour and you have to mentally prepare yourself for whom you are going to deal with, and be able to be with them for an hour on their own terms and adapt to their personality. I like being with different types of people." Alicia wants people to know that she is definitely a friendly person. However, she also wants people to know that she can get "ugly fast."

Alicia also believes that her New York roots will help her in the outback. "New Yorkers are tough; we live in the fastest city in the world with lots and lots of people, and the minute you walk out of your apartment, it's chaos and it's a pressure situation 24/7. I'm definitely going to have an advantage over someone who comes from a small rural town who isn't used to dealing with the pressure of a lot of people, personalities, and emotions." Her job and her hometown will aid her in her quest for survival.

"A big part of *Survivor* is your will to survive; you can do anything if you have to do it and you want to do it. The mental aspect of this is the hardest part; trying to cope with these people you don't know who are probably really going to get on your nerves. It will be a pressure situation; that's what I do in my job every day. I deal with a lot of different people with a lot of different problems and attitudes; when you learn how to diffuse that and adapt to it, it is not so hard. I am definitely a focused person and when I set my mind to something, I definitely can do it, so I'm not worried about surviving out there. I think I have it all together."

MICHAEL

Michael sees himself as "a big mind game person" and will be ruthless, if he has to be, in competition. He sees himself as a leader and sees *Survivor* as a struggle. However, he admits to having a know-it-all personality and loves to pull pranks.

Reflecting on the first show, Michael uses the phrase "staying under the radar screen." "In the first show, several people got a few votes at the very beginning, like Rudy, and then he went for a month without a single vote

because he kind of laid low and stayed under the radar screen. That's going to be my biggest challenge, because I'm an energetic, some people say hyper, guy. I'm gonna want to be in the forefront and I'm gonna want my hands in everything and I'm going to have to sit back a little bit, and that's going to be my biggest struggle."

In applying for *Survivor: The Australian Outback,* Michael's friends told him not to do anything to prepare for it. "I heard about the show and it sounded quite a bit up my alley from a survivor standpoint, because I'm a big hunter and I love the challenge of the game; I'm a big mind games person. My children dragged me into the first interview."

Michael says that he believes that he has the tools to be a player in the series. "I know that when I play a board game or if I play Pictionary, I use whatever tools that I can use to win, and I don't feel any remorse afterwards. I'm friends with everybody that I started playing with during the beginning, but during the game sometimes you have to be a little creative or devious."

The main thing he learned from the last show is that too many people got caught up in the fact that they did not want to do something that went against their normal way and it affected their decisions.

Regarding what it will take to win, Michael says, "What it is gonna take to win is gonna be good character, since the flawed character will become evident right away, and since the alliance thing will be on the top of everybody's mind from the very start, the insincere characters will show up pretty quickly. After forty days, you are gonna be yourself, no matter how hard you try not to be, or no matter what you portray yourself as, so you might as well start from the beginning that way, and I think that I am a pretty likable guy."

Regarding hiding his personality, Michael says, "You gotta be yourself, but you have to make sure that the dominant part of your personality does not come across too forcefully to people that may not be able to handle it."

Also regarding being controlling, Michael says, "I was told through extensive psychological testing that I was a control person, and I never thought I was a control person until I was told that, so wanting to take charge of something might be an issue with people."

Michael believes that this show, including the Challenges, will be far more competitive than the last one. He believes that it will be a very big challenge to remain on the show. Already planning ahead, Michael says, "I gotta make sure that I let the people who need sleep get their sleep. I have to go find an area where I can be awake and not disrupt anybody, unless it's prank time."

Pranks are a part of Michael and have been with him all his life. "I have one of those pasts where I got into a lot of trouble. I'm a trouble-maker from way back when, and I'm still a troublemaker. My trouble-making is endearing to some people, and not so endearing to other people. The pranks that I am well-known for are usually taken cheer-fully, but after forty days with no food and little rest, they could proba-bly get on people's nerves."

Kimmi

Kimmi is adamant about her chances on *Survivor: The Australian Out-back.* "I'm coming out to *Survivor* to kick butt!" The thought of a mil-lion dollars to Kimmi was not the motivation. To her, it was just the personal challenge to the people at home who say she is flighty and just a dreamer. "In the beginning, it is an adventure, but in the end it is a game, and that's when you have to buckle down and get serious with everybody, and prove to everybody, including myself, that this is a per-

sonal thing to me. I am going to prove to my-self that, yes, I can do this. I'm not passionate about many things, but this is something that I am passionate about, and it will take me where I need to go."

Kimmi admits that she is not in a rush to join the rat race. "I'm twenty-seven years old and I don't have an office job...*wheeew!*" Kimmi is having fun and, she says, "everybody goes to the Hamptons to party, and I'm the one who helps them have a good time."

Reflecting on last season's *Survivor,* Kimmi absolutely loved Sue, Rich, and Rudy. In pre-paration for the competition in the outback, she has been fattening up; "I've been getting chubby," she says. Kimmi be-lieves that she will be in disguise as a "gay, overweight man." However, she predicts that she will make more than one alliance. Kimmi also calls herself a procrastinator so she says that she will decide when she gets there how she will play the game.

Kimmi is also a bit impatient in some respects. "I have no tolerance for stupidity. If you keep making the same mistake over and over again, I'll make you cry if I have to. I know it sounds horrible. If you are sitting there trying to get blood from a stone and it's not happening, well, it ain't gonna happen tomorrow if it didn't happen yesterday. It didn't happen today, it isn't happening tomorrow, so just stop already. You want blood from a stone, I'll knock it over your head."

Because of her job as a bartender, Kimmi will be able to read people very well. "I am a chameleon, I think. I'm good at judging people because of my job; I get to see people in action and read them. I see the games people play and I'm going to play and hopefully beat everyone."

Also regarding her work as a bartender, Kimmi says, "Bartending, I'm the center of attention. There's me and maybe one or two other people behind the bar with me. You have the masses in front of you and there could be three hundred people screaming in the area around you and you're the target. They want this, they want that. They are throwing their money at you and I can handle that. I don't have a problem with that, so being with strangers, I'll talk to anyone, because I get bored if I do not talk to anyone." Her people skills will help her, but Kimmi says, "you cannot judge a person in one or two days, and that's what's going to be real rough, because people that you are drawn to might be the worst people in the world you want to know."

Kimmi admits to "being like every other woman" in that she gets emotional. When she votes someone off, she will feel bad because it is like hurting somebody. However, she says that if she gets the itch to do something, she will have to do it. Kimmi likes to portray herself as a person who tries her best. "Fail or succeed, as long as you tried something you believed in. The message is just give it your best."

Kimmi wants the others to see her for what she is: "I have a big mouth, I'm adventurous, I'm spontaneous, I'm a goofball, I'm a knucklehead, I have a good heart and I think that's what people will see from me. I mean well." However, she says she will just sit there and if everyone else wants to flake out, she will flake out with the best of them until the end. She says, "I can sit there and make fun of the best of them, but I can make fun of myself as well. I am an equal opportunity insulter."

Kimmi believes that "common sense is not as common as they say it is. I have to live with myself every single day and my family has to live with what I do. The American public will forget everything after a while anyway. Monica Lewinsky and the president is old news. Let her sell handbags, and let him keep doing what he wants to do, because society is very forgiving. If we all look in the mirror, we are all messed up."

Ogakor Tribe

MITCHELL

Mitchell's main goal is to maintain the fun as long as possible. He believes he will be initially observant and read people. Mitchell will keep the people he'd like to hang out with on the island by forming or joining an alliance. "I think the smartest thing to do is to go and read the people, but not for too long, because you don't want to be left out of any alliances that might form. I think you have to get a good feel of what people are thinking, what they are looking at, what they are looking toward, and then decide who to approach, because if you approach somebody who is anti-alliance, well, you have pretty much crapped in your own nest right there, so you have to be careful who you are talking to."

Mitchell thinks that no matter who is on the team, they will lose competitions and not have enough food. He says, "We are gonna go hungry, no matter who we keep on there, we are gonna win some Challenges and lose some Challenges no matter who is with us. I want to keep the people I want to be with; the cooler people, that's who I want to be with."

Mitchell applied for the first *Survivor.* Looking back on the last season, though he did not identify with anyone, Mitchell was rooting for Sue. He thought that she was pretty funny, and because she was from the Midwest, he rooted for her. However, Sue surprised him at the end. This year he thinks everyone should do things in moderation: "Don't be preaching your Bible, running around naked, playing the ukelele, or whatever."

Mitchell wants to have more fun than the group did last time. He says, "I felt like last time they started out with a lot of energy, but it quickly died, and I'm sure it had a lot to do with the heat and lack of food, and things like that, but I hope to maintain it longer. I want to have fun more than anything."

However, this time around, Mitchell believes that the competition will be more physical than mental. He also believes that last time alliances played the bigger part. This time, he thinks that it might be the Challenges. "I think they've got something in store for us and I'm a little worried." Also, he hopes that the producers try their best to make it safe, but he knows that they cannot take away the dangers of the land,

because the spiders and things like that can creep in at any time. In preparing for *Survivor* Mitchell says, "I really can't think of anything in my life to prepare me for what I'm about to do, I guess, except that I can be pretty witty and outwit some of them. I hope that I am younger than most of them."

In talking about himself and his life, Mitchell says, "I'm not an angry person. I never have a bad day and I never look at a day and say 'that sucked'; I don't get down or stressed out about things. I'm usually always as I am right now. I do not change that often."

Moving to the New York area, Mitchell thought people would keep to themselves when it came to his height. However, they are very happy to approach him every single day of his life. People usually ask him how tall he is, or if he plays basketball. It took Mitchell a little while to adjust to life in New York City. "It took at least six months to get used to the people and the way to dress. At first I wore plaids, and people asked where I was from—I had to pick up the pace."

TINA

In thinking ahead, Tina says her plan will be to kick off the mean, bossy people first, but "in a nice way." She calls her strategy "the self-preservation plan": it involves kicking off the weakest first until the merger, and then voting off the threatening, strong people. Tina says, "I have thought about my strategy and it's changed a couple of times, so I am still not sure which one I'm gonna go with, but I thought if you kick off all the mean, hateful, snotty, nasty people, then maybe you'll be left with all the good people, so you are gonna have a party as soon as you get rid of all the mean, hateful, nasty people." Tina continues with her description of her plan by saying: "We start out with two tribes. I think it's important to survive as a tribe, so we have to kick off the weakest people athletically, or

those who would cause us to lose Challenges. Then, when we combine the tribes, and it got down to it, and we couldn't vote off the mean, hateful, snotty people, then I would probably try to vote the people that were a threat to me in Challenges."

Tina really looks forward to the adventures and Challenges. She will strive to be competitive in all the Challenges because she wants to hold her integrity intact. That is why she will vote people off in a "nice" way.

Tina realizes that *Survivor* is a game, but she also knows that she is a competitive person. If she were to win, she says it would be because of her competitive nature. She says, "To me, it's more about the adventure of it all, and less about the money and coming out on top."

Reflecting on the last show, Tina related to Colleen and Sean the most. To Tina, they played nice, just as she wants to. "I think this game can be played very nicely, kindly, and sweetly, and a good example of that is Sean and Colleen. They stayed nice to people and you didn't hear them be real ugly to other people." If Tina were playing last year, she would have wanted to be in the Pagong tribe, because she would have been miserable in Tagi.

For the outback, Tina plans to do her very best because "my motto in life is to live a life less ordinary. I feel like you only do this once, and I want to do it to the best of my ability. I want to do it hard and fast and just suck it in, because I really believe you only get this one chance." For Tina, *Survivor* is a "life-changing, altering experience. I don't think I will be a different person by any means. It's just a stop along the way on my journey of living this life less ordinary."

She says that she has a very high metabolism and that she never has been hungry. "To be honest," she says, however, "I've never gone more than twenty-four hours without eating."

JERRI

This will be Jerri's second attempt at being on *Survivor,* and this time she really had a good time editing her audition tape. Jerri always has to keep reminding herself that *Survivor* is a game. She admits to being a control freak, and says she has already bitten her nails off in anticipation of the game. To find a way of not being so controlling, Jerri believes that she will be meditating. She also believes that it will be like a chess game and it will take some cunning behavior to get into the right situation. People will race to be in an alliance. However, this time around, it will have to happen quicker, because "you don't want to be left out." In fact, one of Jerri's favorite books, a gift from a friend, is *The 48 Laws of Power.* The book has suddenly come in handy for her, as it has a lot to do with interacting with a lot of people, the struggle for power, and the different ways to gain power and mingle with people.

Growing up as an army brat, Jerri moved around a lot, and that has made her into the person she is today. Her family moved every couple of years, forcing Jerri into new situations in unfamil-

iar environments filled with strangers. "You definitely learn to make friends at a very accelerated pace."

Looking back on the first season of *Survivor*, Jerri related to Colleen Haskell the most, and her strategy of being quiet initially and staying in the background. At the same time, she also admired the strength of Kelly and Gretchen.

On evaluating herself, Jerri does not consider herself a conniving person.

"I'm not the type of person that likes to step on other people or hurt other people's feelings, but it is a game." Jerri was attracted to the outback because she loves the desert and does a lot of backpacking, hiking, and swimming. "It's putting me back in the atmosphere that I'm most comfortable in."

However, as much as the outdoor environment is challenging to Jerri, the mind games will be more challenging. "This is definitely more of a people situation, which is more difficult and more challenging than the outdoor environment, but I have been reading a lot about Australia, and there's a lot of freaky things going on over there, and they are really insane. The crocodile stories alone are '*whoa!*'"

COLBY

Colby is very excited at the prospect of going to the outback and he is "ready to go." Colby did not relate to anyone on the first show. He will not have a strategy until he gets there. However, he does know that he wants to think quickly and relate to people; listen more than talk. "You have got to be able to relate to people, and I think the best way to relate to someone is to listen to them, and I plan to do a lot more listening than talking." He does not intend on volunteering a lot of information about himself or what his plans are, because he says there is no need for that. "You become the Captain America figure by standing out and doing the things that give you that perception, so, the simple answer to that is don't do all those things. I don't have to feed my ego by standing out in this thing."

He is cautious about crossing the line from being an asset to being a threat and he is especially concerned about this with regard to men. "The male thing is probably going to be tougher for me. I have an easy time talking to females and relating to them and communicating with them. Honestly, I am worried more about the males because of the threat thing. I

don't know why that's more on my mind at this point than worrying about a band of women voting me off."

Colby sees his strength as a leader and being able to take control of situations. However, he says that he does not necessarily have to lead from the front of the pack, as do most leaders. When the time comes for someone to truly step up and take control, he plans to be the one, but there might be others. "We are there to win. If you have four leaders and four followers, or one leader and seven followers, then things fit into place easily. If you have eight leaders, then there's instant conflict."

Colby says that he has to be diverse in the way he handles things and the way he handles people. However, Colby says his weakness is "not being able to play the Indian instead of the chief." Colby says that he will need to know when to play the Indian.

KEL

Kel's plan is that he'll refuse to answer direct questions. He also believes alliances are all right—a "necessary evil"—and that he will choose one within the first three days. Looking back on the last *Survivor*, Kel related to Gretchen because he admired her integrity. "Gretchen—what an outstanding individual with physical strength, yet [she] brought a level of integrity to the game. I'm going to play the same way Gretchen did, but I am going to develop alliances. It's a necessary evil; you can't survive the game without having alliances, that's just the way it is.

"My father and I have talked to each other several times about the strategy; we talked about a timetable of when I am going to do this and who I am going to make alliances with.

"When I develop these alliances with people, I want them to feel that once they make these agreements with me, I'm gonna carry them

through. If I make an agreement with someone, I will stand by it.

"I am going to have to decide who are my allies, and who are the people I can trust, and who are going to be my enemies. I've already started playing. Right when we started to do the interviews, you walk by the contestants and you overhear conversations; I've been taking some notes."

Of all the contestants, Kel seems to identify most with adventure. "There's two reasons I applied. Obviously, the adventure and also the money; it is very simple, I love adventure but I also want the million dollars. Adventure is what sold me on the military. I got into the military at a late age of twenty-eight, so I know how to relate to civilians; it won't be hard whatsoever to step back into that civilian mode again." Having said that, Kel foresees potential conflict. "From being in the military, I have a tendency to wake up at 5:30 or 6:00 for physical training. Maybe my early morning wake-ups will bother people."

KEITH

Keith has his own special plan. It is called "the stomach strategy." He says that he is not likely to join an alliance, and will take it day by day. Keith is very confident, but he is not sure that alliances will work this time and he will have a hard time being a backstabber.

Keith's strategy relies a lot on his ability to cook and cook well. "I'm a cook and I've done a lot of cooking, and I think my resourcefulness as a cook can help feed everybody and help everybody be comfortable. I'm gonna be very much the team leader in the sense of listen, let's get every-body fed and comfortable so we can win these Immunity Challenges. Being a chef is a tough job. Everybody who eats in a restaurant should walk back in the kitchen, shake the chef's hand and say 'I commend you for what you do.'" For Keith, his life as a restaurateur and chef has built within him some survival techniques. Keith says, "In general, my life has kind of a survivor quality. I think I get along with people very well; I have an extremely long fuse, and I'm a good sport when I lose, and I don't think I'm going to take it so seriously that it's gonna affect my performance."

Keith will take it day by day and he will make no predictions. "I'll take no quarter and I'll give no quarter. The cards have been dealt, fate is inevitable. I dedicate this time to my kids, Josh and Alicia, and I'm just gonna do the best I can do."

Upon reflection on last season's show, Keith had a tremendous amount of respect for Rudy as a player (especially for his age). To Keith, Rudy was far from weak. He says, "I think all of us that are playing have some level of confidence or we wouldn't be playing this game. *Survivor* is not for the meek or mild individual, because you gotta have something inside you that says 'I think I can get to the finish.'" However, Keith admits that the competition will surely get ugly and if he gets voted off, he will be happy that he had the opportunity and that he had a great time.

Regarding Richard Hatch and the million dollar prize, Keith says, "Did Richard do the wrong thing? Some people said he did the wrong thing. Well, his bank account has a million dollars in it, so I guess he did the right thing."

Being a chef and knowing food is Keith. "Why would you kill the cook? Keep him around; who's gonna cook Thanksgiving dinner? It's Keith, he's not going anywhere; so that's the plan, because I'm not much of a ruthless, conniving, backstabbing-type person, which you pretty much have to be in order to win this thing." Keith's plan is to be the useful, resourceful, adventurous, "I'm your buddy" kind of guy.

"I'm gonna feed you and you'll be good with me."

Keith plans to use his skills as a chef in the outback. "Australia has some fantastic ingredients, and hopefully as a chef I can source them and do something with them—beau monde, wattle seed, you have got lemon myrtle—great items; it's whether or not I can source them, find them in the right season and create a method for cooking them and doing something with them that's a little different and unusual. So, I'm envisioning bouillabaisse, paellas, and etoufées and gumbos. Let's do something a little creative and that will be my challenge. I'm thinking stews; I'm seeing stews . . . yam stews with wichita grub; tastes like chicken."

MARALYN

Maralyn believes her police skills and mental strength will help her outwit others. She plans to be manipulative without letting others see what she's doing. Maralyn related to Rudy in the first show, and feels she has the same life experience that will make her a similar success. "I really liked Rudy, I swear to God, what a crusty guy, but a man of real substance. Surviving on the beat on a daily basis for any kind of cop gives the word 'survivor' new meaning. Physically, when I was a captain

in charge of a whole section, and we go out there during a midnight tour, my goal was that all of my people got to check off in one piece. That, in my opinion, was a successful tour of duty, and I was grateful for that. [Survivor] will really put me through the test of how tough I am in the mental department, because this is a mental game more than anything else." She laughs when she thinks of her tendency to swear. "I will probably be the one who is the most bleeped. Some people are going to like me, some people won't; some folks I'm gonna like, some not so naturally. I'm going to gravitate to people that like me."

Maralyn has a hard shell, and feels that many will be surprised at her compassion for animals, while marveling at the hard way she plays the game. "When I see my first kangaroo…the symbol of Australia… I'm gonna lose it. I don't think I am a threatening person; anyone who can cry over a kangaroo—*hello!*" She feels there should be a women's alliance this time, "a.k.a. a 'battle of the bitches.' This could be a 'queen of the flies' this time, as opposed to lord of the flies. We'd save the good men for last. We have to hang onto our strong, good men to win those Challenges. Then hey, it'll be a battle of the bitches."

AMBER

Amber comes from a Catholic family and goes to church every Sunday. She applied because she did not want to get a permanent job after college, as everyone else was doing. Amber's boyfriend is still in school and her parents are very excited for her, but also very jealous.

Looking back on the first show, Amber related to Colleen and Greg the most, calling Greg "wonderful." She watched every week and got all her family and friends interested.

Amber appears to be a sweet, innocent girl but she says that her conniving side will show toward the middle of the show. "I'm not going to come out being blatantly mean, but they are going to know that I'm not the sweet, innocent girl that they can take advantage of. I'm not going to let them."

Amber plans to try to relate to each player on a personal level. "Have every person relate to me in a different way, and hopefully I can find out something about them. When they find out something about me, I can then relate to them on a personal level, so, in the beginning they will want me there and won't want to kick me off."

Amber also plans to switch personalities halfway through by being tough initially, but then laid-back after the merger. Despite being laid-back, she says she will remain conniving. She says people do not realize that she has a couple of mean bones in her body and that they will help her get through it.

Sixteen Strategies for Winning *Survivor*

Now that the contestants have had their say, here's a list of the best and worst strategies for playing *Survivor.*

1. The Entertainer

The Entertainer strategy is thus: be the life of the party, make everyone laugh, be so incredibly charming that everyone falls in love with you. It's the old high school class clown strategy. In any large group of people, one will adopt the role of Entertainer. What happens next depends on how entertaining and endearing they really are. During a show like *Survivor,* this is a very bold strategy to adopt because it makes the individual visible to the group—and keeps them that way—for better or worse. Diehard extroverts who sing show tunes at the drop of a hat and love throwing dinner parties for a hundred can't help but adopt this strategy. They live life this way, is their explanation, and can't imagine behaving differently.

Positives: The good Entertainers—the men and women who use this strategy with a touch of nuance, knowing when to turn on their charms and when to shut them down and get real— stand a brilliant chance of winning *Survivor.* This is a very likable person, someone we all feel close to whether we are or not. It helps if they're good listeners, striving competitors. People like this form alliances almost by default, drawing friends about them and making them feel like they've known each other forever. Casting a vote against a secure individual who is a good Entertainer is incredibly difficult, and usually a last resort.

A good example of this was Sonja from the first *Survivor.* She wasn't halfway to the island on Day One before she was breaking out her ukulele. Talk about your risky moves. In the hands of a more obtrusive individual, that little piece of wood and string would've become firewood by nightfall. But Sonja was charming, intelligent, a sensitive listener, and everyone's image of their favorite aunt— the one who brought tons of presents every time she came to visit. In the end, though, that proved her undoing. Everyone loved Sonja so much they couldn't stand to see her suffer. There was a consensus that the island would be too hard on her. When she fell down during the first Im-

munity Challenge, that suspicion was reinforced. When Rudy said that voting Sonja off was like "putting down your favorite dog," it may have sounded callous, but it wasn't. Rudy was saying that if Sonja were younger and stronger she would have had a place on the island. Everyone loved her.

Negatives: Unless they're physically gifted and temporarily necessary to a tribe's survival, the bad Entertainer can face immediate dismissal. People look for reasons to vote this person off instead of reasons to keep him or her around. Bad Entertainers don't know when to turn it off, and think everyone loves their jokes, even the tenth time around. People hate bad Entertainers: they talk too much, applaud themselves too much, behave inappropriately, and say sappy things like "I love you," even when they can't remember your first name. They remind everyone of their psychotic uncle with the comb-over, the one with the blue ruffles and velvet bow tie on his tux shirt, who makes a living singing covers of songs like "Feelings" and "My Way" at a Denny's off the Strip in Vegas. The bad Entertainer is such an obnoxious, cloying individual that he or she would have a hard time winning *Survivor.*

2. The Leader

Every group needs a leader, and sooner or later someone steps forth to take control. But this strategy isn't about leadership by default. This strategy is practiced by those men and women who feel it their God-given right to take charge. The Leader's quest for power is ingrained, whether through genetics or dysfunction, and is used during the *Survivor* game at the Leader's peril. Assuming command is, as the Aussies say, becoming a "tall poppy." The theory goes that in any field of poppies, one or two poppies will grow taller than all the rest. The other poppies will get jealous and do whatever they can to cut the tall poppies down to size.

So it is in *Survivor.* Leaders are almost begging to get voted off. Taking command of a small tribe is a delicate operation, something for which blustery Leaders are often ill-equipped. They speak in loud voices, stand tall, and tend to be critical.

However, they are also vital. Without the Leader, a tribe will be without focus, just like any society or organization without leadership. The alpha male sees that things happen in an orderly way. They instill a pecking order. They build group pride. But can they win *Survivor*? The first time around, B.B. played this role. Though he got voted off early, there's every reason to believe he could have done very well if he had lasted longer. He was adapting to the environment and softening his tone. His resolve to lead was diminished by the Pagong tribe's apathy, but he was still an achiever. It stands to reason that if a subversive authority figure like Richard can win the game, a standup authority figure can win too. Still, a dicey strategy, this.

Positives: Everybody loves a winner. And men and women with leadership skills are often perceived as being winners. For the Leader with confidence, polish, good looks, and the physical strength to win an Immunity Challenge or two, this strategy could be extremely effective. Think of it as *Survivor*'s version of hanging out with the most popular kid in the schoolyard—everyone wants to be like him, everyone wants to be his friend, his word is law (though he never shoves that point down anyone's throat; rather, he greases the point with a hearty smile and a wink).

One plus about this version of the Leader strategy: the man or woman with the charisma to pull it off and win *Survivor* is almost guaranteed lasting fame. America will be drawn to that individual.

Negatives: Playing the part of dictator. Benevolent or not, a dictator engenders animosity because he makes others feel powerless. Turning *Survivor* into a personal banana republic (the metaphorical nation, not the clothing store) may make an individual feel powerful for a short while, but that's destined to be short-lived. Fellow contestants will meet furtively, in ones and twos, then in larger groups, to discuss how much they revile this person. Expulsion can be as swift as the next Tribal Council. *Survivor*'s secret electoral process means a dictatorial leader can be voted off without repercussion.

3. The Flirt

A troublesome strategy because of its sexual overtones, and feeble because it makes the perpetrator reliant upon others. Simply, this man or woman bats eyelashes as a reminder to someone powerful that great

things are soon to come. The Flirt must be cute and attractive. If ugly, the individual must be confident. The Flirt must be smart enough to plan ahead. Intelligence should be hidden while playing the Flirt, however, because it will threaten the very people it was meant to deceive. These people will claim they've been manipulated, and be cautious of any future flirtatious advances.

Positives: A bold beginning. The intelligent Flirt makes the most of the first week of contestant life, when people of the opposite (or perhaps same) sex are feeling frisky. Bewitching is easy. The smart Flirt uses this time to make friends, build alliances any way possible, then slip into a more lasting strategy (perhaps the Determined Victim, see number 4) on the march to victory.

Negatives: Unless executed by a pro, the Flirt strategy wears thin quickly. A Flirt does well in civilization because they can bat and run. Each night they leave the office, leaving the object of flirtation to wonder about them through the night. The next morning the Flirt returns to the office, showered, freshly coiffed, and wearing something appropriately flirtatious.

However, the Flirt is seen in all his or her glory each and every minute of *Survivor*. Fellow contestants see them tired, disheveled, and snoring. A Flirt who's gone three weeks without a shower or toothbrush seems unappealing.

The Flirt who cannot maneuver into a more mature fallback strategy after *Survivor*'s first week is potentially flirting with failure.

4. The Determined Victim (a.k.a. the Underdog)

This potent cocktail of a strategy could be a winner. The Determined Victim is the defiant yet lovable misfit that will compete harder, sleep less, and display surprising pools of emotional depth. Their work ethic will be tireless. They may come across as insecure initially, but soon the tribe will see that the Determined Victim is playful and gregarious—if given the chance. That's all the Determined Victim ever asks from life.

The victim aspect guarantees underestimation by fellow contestants, meaning no one sees the Determined Victim as a threat (threats get voted off). The determined part means fellow contestants respect the competitive spirit, a handy attribute for Challenges. Combined, the two have "individual" written all over, meaning fellow contestants consider this man or woman incapable of forging alliances.

In principle, the Determined Victim owns heroic qualities of mythic proportion. They have overcome long years of being beaten down by looking deep inside themselves and finding greatness. Their quest to realize that greatness inspires those around them.

Positives: In reality, few such people exist, and those that do can be insufferable (see *Negatives*). Lucky for them, the ideal of the Determined Victim has been fodder for thousands of inspirational movies (*Rocky*, *Rudy*, etc.). We are societally programmed to root for these people instead of voting them off. Those men and women savvy enough to affect—and it is an affectation of the total-commitment variety—this persona in an endearing manner will find others admiring them.

Negatives: The reality of actually being a Determined Victim. Despite what modern society says, nobody likes a victim. They whine, they're feeble, are quick to blame, they abdicate all responsibility for their personal well-being to whomever will take it. And determined? On a victim that behavior comes across as pushy (best-case scenario) or moronic (typical occurrence).

5. The Professor

Another brilliant strategy, and just as tough to pull off. The Professor is the resident genius, and every group of contestants needs one in their new home. The Professor makes them feel that someone really, really smart has the answers to all their problems. Things will be built, broken things will be fixed, food will be procured, fresh water will be distilled from whatever briny mess the contestants confront. The Professor will be an individual of common sense. He or she will have the answer to every question. When a sudden squall wipes out the camp and every contestant feels downtrodden (and sodden), the Professor will rub his or her hands together with glee, anticipating the joy of rebuilding. Life is an experiment to the Professor, and the answer is always out there.

Positives: The Professor is indispensable. The savvy Professor will add to his intellect by displaying likability, in the form of

showing others how to do simple tasks like lashing eucalyptus branches properly, or building an ingenious fish
trap. However, since arcane scientific knowledge is his
forte (and *Survivor* insurance policy) he won't appear a
bad guy by withholding tidbits like water distillation and
the secret of cold fusion from the tribe. They'll figure it's
out of their intellectual realm.

Negatives: One word—madcap. O.K., one more—anal. Professors
are right-brain thinkers, a group known for preferring
method over compassion. Sometimes a Professor can live
too much inside his own head, increasing other's perception of him as a loony dingbat. It won't help if the Professor lacks physical fitness, for a combination of brawn and
intellect are crucial to *Survivor*.

6. The Zealot

Why bother showing up? The Zealot's fanaticism, whether about religion, a sports team, or physical fitness, is often a one-way ticket
off *Survivor*. The Zealot's world is all black or white, no grays. There is
nothing intrinsically unlikable about these people, they're just broken
records. They try to talk about something else, but they're predisposed to
fanaticism. They'll even trade one fixation for another. When pressed,
the Zealot will admit their life has been a string of fanatic beliefs. Maybe
it started with partying, the absolute best parties, the most intense. Their
whole lives revolved around partying. Then it became physical fitness.
The Zealot worked out several hours a day, every day. Diet came next.
The Zealot became a food nazi. Finally, religion or sports or politics. And
the list goes on. Survivors don't.

Positives: The ability to fixate. Fixating on *Survivor* is a great way to
win. The smart Zealot will tell his other fixations to be
quiet during his contestant tenure. He or she will throw all
their energy into developing a smart *Survivor* strategy.
Their experience with laser-like focus will allow them to
explore every nuance of the game. No other Survivor—
save a fellow Zealot—will be able to match their awareness. If the Zealot is a team player, blessed with physical
talent, and imbued with a certain flair, there's even a possibility they'll last long enough to stop fixating on external
beliefs and begin the painful work of listening to his or her

fellow contestants' points of view. That touch of empathy, combined with zeal for the game, could be a winner.

Negatives: Where to start? Being stranded on *Survivor* with a Zealot is like being seated next to the know-it-all at the dinner party from hell. Contestants will run, not walk, to vote this individual back to civilization.

7. The Mom

This is a gender-specific strategy (the Dad often comes across as being number 2, The Leader). The Mom is a beautiful person on the inside; it doesn't hurt if she looks good in khaki shorts, either. She is maternal in the best possible way, nudging the younger members of the tribe (a dysfunctional family for the ages) to act as civilized as possible. For older members, she is caring but firm, not allowing them to become curmudgeonly. She cooks, she builds, she organizes, she sleeps little, she complains even less. The Mom has seen it all and is surprised by little. And the best part of all for a Survivor willing to adopt the Mom strategy: it comes naturally. No play-acting for this role.

The Mom in the first *Survivor* was Gretchen. Her warmth and humor kept the Pagong tribe from self-destructing, and her maternal affection towards Greg was so strong that she postponed flying back to civilization after being voted off so that she could learn Greg's fate. An example of the power of the Mom strategy came after Gretchen was voted off: not only were her fellow contestants stunned, but members of the production crew were emotionally devastated. There was a pall over the production compound afterward, as if some vital element had left the game.

Positives: Voting Mom off is like the ultimate act of betrayal, and few fellow contestants are willing to do this. It hits too close to their insecurities of being alone, far from home. The Mom is a reassuring presence. To last on *Survivor,* a good Mom should be young enough to display physical stamina but old enough that she commands respect. Say early forties. The Mom can use her knowledge of relationship skills to build alliances and maintain tenuous friendships.

Negatives: Somewhere, back in the real world, the Mom has kids of her own. Being away for six weeks is a huge strain. There might also be a generation gap in the tribe, with younger

members allying to oust an individual who comes across as too matronly or overbearing. Also, playing the Mom has the additional liability of Freudian overtones. Men and women will reflect on relationships with their own mother, acting out these emotions against the Mom. Strange stuff, and seemingly out of place in the wilderness, but yet another proof that *Survivor*'s focus is social survival.

8. The Athlete

This is a strategy one inherits through genetics, but it's sound and successful. The Athlete commands instant *Survivor* respect. The tribe will think this person indispensable upon arrival in their new home, a belief that will be reinforced by performance in the usually physical Immunity Challenges. The Athlete has the added bonus of having been athletic all his or her life, a highly desirable quality in society. There's a certain public adoration that goes along with being an Athlete. He or she has felt it and is made more confident by it.

Part of being an Athlete is a bit of sex appeal, too. The male Athlete isn't afraid of taking his shirt off when the weather's hot (nor is the bold woman) or of walking around in shorts. Their physical movements are coordinated and graceful, often making those around them look awkward by comparison. Their lifetime of being the Athlete has made them embrace activity in all its guises, which means that many—not all, for the Athlete has also been taught to conserve energy for vital competitions—are hard workers.

Positives: The Athlete is guaranteed a free pass through the game's First Act. He or she becomes a leader by default, is indispensable in Immunity Challenges, vital for hauling heavy lumber and plants for home building, and a rallying point for fellow contestants. There's something reassuring about being in the presence of a dominant individual. This is a primal urge. In nature, a male version of this takes place with the silverback gorillas of Rwanda. Female ringtail lemurs of Madagascar are similarly dominant. And while nature doesn't allow gorillas or lemurs the option of voting off a leader they've become disgruntled with, it's unlikely their tribes would do such a thing unless the rules of existence change.

Same goes for the Athlete. Their physical dominance and subsequent leadership becomes a currency buying them time in the *Survivor* game. Their ingrained competitive skills may easily lead them to victory.

Negatives: Unlike the gorilla or lemur's environment, that of the Athlete changes. By the end of Act One, an Athlete must minimize his or her physical strength lest it become a threat to others. He or she must develop endearing personality skills. Political savvy, something the Athlete has always confused with charisma or charm, becomes vital. The Athlete that does not adapt to the changes wrought by Act Two will soon be voted off.

9. The Wild and Crazy Guy (or Girl)

Different from the Entertainer but often bearing the same traits, the Wild and Crazy Guy or Girl drifts in and out of the tribe's consciousness, depending upon his or her mood. They're not always on and can often be moody. They think themselves deep thinkers and capable of sweeping emotion, but keep that to themselves, preferring to paint an image of carefree craziness. The Wild and Crazy person likes to do and say outrageous things. The Wild and Crazy Guy or Girl is their identity back in the real world, so their behavior on the island isn't an act or change of pace. Rather, knowing the stakes are higher, the Wild and Crazy person acts even wilder and crazier. No stunt is too bizarre, no comment too outrageous.

The Wild and Crazy Guy or Girl, however, deeply craves acceptance. This is his or her Achilles heel. Since the very notion of *Survivor* revolves around which people are acceptable to a group and which are not, playing the game is almost a sado-masochistic exercise for the Wild and Crazy person. They know from past experience that they have the right stuff to make people laugh and to entertain a group. He or she also knows that the odds of total acceptance on *Survivor* (defined as victory) are one in sixteen—not great odds.

Positives: As long as the Wild and Crazy person works and competes hard in Immunity Challenges, he or she will be guaranteed a long stay on *Survivor*. Every group in a harsh environment needs a touch of levity. Despite using antics as a means of procuring attention, the Wild and Crazy person is more emotionally balanced than the Entertainer.

This allows him or her to gradually cease being Wild and Crazy all the time, and slowly work into the framework of the tribe. The Wild and Crazy person's time in the spotlight makes them natural leaders if people will follow. By combining a strategy of levity with quiet leadership (defined as quietly making suggestions that others will follow, instead of announcing "I'm in charge"), the Wild and Crazy Guy or Girl can have a deep emotional impact on the game. Maybe, with a little physical ability thrown in, he or she can win.

Negatives: Wild and Crazy Guys or Girls that act too needy flame out fast. No contestant wants to spend forty-two days soothing someone else's fragile ego. Also, eccentric behavior can be a tension reliever sometimes, but downright annoying at others. The Wild and Crazy person who tries too hard to be funny, act outrageous, and be the center of attention is one of the most annoying types of people on earth. In *Survivor*'s close environment, that tired act won't play for long. Finally, Wild and Crazy people lacking the ability to blend with others will have to resort to winning Immunity each and every Challenge in order to avoid being voted off. They may be comfortable with this—as loners, they're used to self-sufficiency—but it's insane to imagine one person winning Immunity all the time.

10. The Quiet One

Ah, brilliance. The Quiet One is clean and neat and nondescript. He or she doesn't give orders or offer opinions. There is boldness in this person's heart, for why else would they apply to become a *Survivor*? But they don't assert this boldness in any way, shape, or form. This doesn't make them meek. They're merely quiet and polite (never rude), which means other contestants don't get offended by their presence. Indeed, half the time they forget the Quiet One exists. The Quiet One uses terms like "flying below the radar" and "being mellow," when what they really mean is "I want to win a million dollars."

Quiet Ones with the physical coordination to win Challenges can write their own ticket late in the game, meaning no one can vote them off. If the Quiet One makes it to the final two, he or she has a good chance of winning. After all, the Quiet One has never offended anyone. In fact, the Quiet One likes almost everyone, making it easier to vote for him or her. This is a centered person, bearing little malice or rage. Back in civilization they might be seen as milquetoast for their inoffensive musical tastes and political indifference. But on *Survivor,* those traits are virtues.

Positives: The Quiet One with the right attributes can easily win. That means enough self-confidence to avoid speaking harshly when a simple contestant says something dumb, physical strength to not slow the tribe down during Challenges, and the smarts (something the Quiet One is belatedly credited with) to understand how the game is progressing and play accordingly. The phrase "still waters run deep" applies here, and the individual gains a perception of strength as the game continues.

Negatives: Being perceived as mousy (women) or wimpy (men). Forget "still waters run deep." Once the Quiet One is seen as weak, fellow contestants will either pounce immediately and vote that person off, or worse, keep him or her around as a toy. Think of a cat batting around a mouse before killing it. Even though the Quiet One uses stealth and silence for strategy, he or she has to talk sooner or later. Problems may arise if the time is chosen poorly.

11. Everybody's Friend

It takes a naturally outgoing and diplomatic man or woman to pull this one off. The ability to talk with anyone and everyone, never showing animosity and hastening to soothe ruffled feathers, is vital. This man or woman needs to be confident, for their pleaser mentality may lead others to see them as weak. Stinging barbs will ensue. Witness how Sue and Kelly denigrated Sean during the first show. He was trying his best to be a diplomat, and all it got him was grief.

The mental stress of absorbing those slings and arrows might weigh heavily on someone less resilient than Everybody's Friend. This character, however, shrugs it off, preferring to seek the best in human nature. The live-and-let-live nature of their behavior is actually an emotionally healthy way to survive six tough weeks. In an ideal world we'd all be able to forgive easily and laugh about insults.

Positives: Really powerful people enjoy having Everybody's Friend around. Shakespeare used to include supplicants like this

into his plays for comic relief. Through appeasement and a quick wit, Everybody's Friend avoids getting voted off. The rationale is that they've offended no one (and everyone if they become too obsequious) and can be voted off at any time. No hurry. Everybody's Friend will leave the contest with a positive mental attitude, maybe distrusting people a little more than before, but not much. Can this strategy win *Survivor*? A longshot. The Machiavellian sensibilities needed to win are not found in a single bone of Everybody's Friend. It would take a most freakish act of nature for this person to slip through the cracks to victory. But it can happen. That's another of *Survivor*'s beauties: anything can happen.

Negatives: High profile and a high obsequiousness factor. Everybody's Friend can come across as dim. Their powerlessness easily renders them a pawn or puppet. Too late, they'll realize that trying to please everyone is no way to build alliances. Rendered beholden to the schemers and power barons, Everybody's Friend will be forced to work extra, extra hard to keep everyone happy during the game's final, divisive days. To use another Shakespearean analogy, "To thine own self be true" may be how Everybody's Friend starts the *Survivor* game— everybody does—but by the end they've compromised so many times it takes weeks to get their head screwed on straight again.

12. The Feral Child

This person has overcome adversity her or his whole life, but has never descended into victim status. He or she is proud of not owing anything to anyone. A keen eye for human character flaws allows this person to prey on the weak and not trust the schemers. Actually, the Feral Child trusts no one. Being surrounded by schemers and backstabbers only sharpens their belief that humanity is out to get him or her.

The Feral Child, of course, is not a child, but was so injured early in life that they remain emotionally young. They've lived the life of *Survivor* forever, so the game is just an extension of their day-to-day existence. The rules are so deeply ingrained that *Survivor* feels like child's play—a payday for living as they would live anyway.

OPPOSITE: Jerri

Positives: Long after the game is over, *Survivor* may have changed this person's life for the better. *Survivor* may bring out some humanity and emotional growth in the Feral Child. That sounds a little showy, but people need other people to win *Survivor*. So much attention is paid to the mistrust in the game that people forget *Survivor* revolves around cooperation. The tribal unit is a family (highly dysfunctional and quickly shattering, but a family nonetheless), and for the Feral Child to survive in that family they must drop their guard a little, display trust, and even display vulnerability (a word that makes Feral Children shudder). By actively involving themselves in the group, Feral Children will be able to combine their better survival traits with the socially necessary ability to coexist and trust. This trust is vital to joining an alliance. That's their path to victory.

Negatives: Life has been too hard on this person and it shows. They come across as hard and angry. They try to be upbeat but it comes across forced. Others dislike this person or mistrust this person before they take the chance to get to know them. This builds a buffer that six weeks of *Survivor* may not be able to overcome. The Feral Child can be his or her own self-fulfilling prophecy: hoping against hope to win *Survivor*, but using the ultimate loss as just another example of how the world is against him or her.

13. The Introvert

Life is tough for the Introvert. Almost all his fellow contestants are extroverted and flamboyant. They like to speak freely and prance around full of energy. When it comes time for campfire conversations, those extroverted contestants will pour out every detail of their life stories, not even stopping for a dramatic pause before mentioning masturbation techniques, compelling lovemaking spots, and lengthy oratories on the beauty of the perfect bowel movement.

Not so for the Introvert. He or she is not a prig, and certainly doesn't refrain from the conversation as a means of passing judgment (though it will invariably be seen this way). Introverts just like to be quiet. It's how they stay strong. In fact, the Introvert may not be sitting around that campfire at all, preferring a quiet spot ten feet off, the one with the beautiful view of the moon and stars.

This behavior can make the Introvert an outcast. He or she will have to overcome their strong inner dislike for prolonged group encounters if victory is to happen.

Positives: Still waters run deep. When the Introvert parks him or herself to the side and turns inward, the game and its processes are foremost on his or her mind. While other contestants are babbling about nothing in particular, Introverts have a unique ability to analyze the game and seek a victory strategy.

Another plus is that Introvert's quiet behavior makes them unnoticeable. Every single contestant eventually drops defenses and begins talking a lot, participating in the group. Animosities develop, as they always do. However, the Introvert would never drop his or her guard to become one with the group. The notion is not part of their personality. Try as they might, being part of the group inevitably feels forced and the Introvert retreats again, staying unnoticed. By the time the Introvert gets to the Final Four, when all bets are off, that energy they've stored will come in handy.

Negatives: Society inherently mistrusts the quiet. People wonder what's going on inside the Introvert's head, fearing the worst, that it's some sort of judgmental thought process. Even without a reason to dislike this person, they'll seek to push the Introvert further from the group. This can lead to being voted off.

14. The Redneck

One doesn't have to be white or from the South to use this strategy. Rednecks, to use a single common term, are people who inherently know how to play the game. Their lifelong version of survival has been about concealing their true selves to achieve their goals. Rednecks are easily underestimated.

Positives: The Redneck has a chip on his or her shoulder. When it's concealed beneath a warm grin and compliant nature, this chip leads others to underestimate him or her. And in the big scheme of *Survivor* traits, underestimation stands atop the heap. The smart Redneck plays coy, works the act, quietly uses lifelong survival skills, and stands an excellent chance of winning. An added bonus is that America can relate to the Redneck. There's something patriotic about a plain-spoken person.

Negatives: Well, Rednecks are perceived as hicks. And hicks are mistaken for simpletons. The Redneck who truly fits that bill is easy pickings for smart players.

15. The Slacker

Really, this has got to be the most annoying persona in Survivor lore. The Slacker pretends to care for nothing. They display little emotion, acting supercool under the most intense pressure. They lie under pressure and tell the truth under pressure and no casual observer can tell the difference because the Slacker's face is always a passive mask. The Slacker is generally a nice person in far over their heads, but that doesn't excuse the indifference. In a world of intensity, indifference is the greatest crime.

Here's the fun part: Someday a slacker will win *Survivor*.

Positives: The Slacker is usually young, which often means he or she has physical strength for the Challenges. And while playing simple and feigning indifference, the Slacker was smart enough to have thrown their passion behind a winning *Survivor* application. So they've got intelligence going for them—which is nice. Finally, the Slacker uses passive-aggressiveness as a potent competitive tool. In a marriage, such behavior is manipulative. But on *Survivor*, passive-aggressive freaks exude an aura of control.

Negatives: The Slacker must get down on their knees and pray with all their might that they do not spend the first three days of their Survivor existence as a member of a tribe dominated by baby boomers and geriatrics. The Slacker would be voted off so quickly by that group, it wouldn't even be funny.

16. The Snake

This was the winning strategy for Richard Hatch. He embodied everything people believe about oily, underhanded individuals. He lied, he cheated, he walked around naked (don't forget that Sean referred to

Richard's tactic as the FNF, or Fat Naked Fag, play), he voted off nice people, and he boldly quit the Hands on the Hard Idol Challenge because he was aware of his unlikability quotient.

Was Richard a good person? Actually, he played evil on TV, but he was great fun to be around and always had something interesting to say. Will Richard's plan work a second time? Maybe, but probably not. It stands to reason that the new batch of contestants will sniff out the Snake and tell him it's time to go home, ASAP.

Positives: Sadly, this is how people survive in the real world. Like good poker players, good snakes keep their hand hidden. They know how to remain stoic when their strategy is falling apart, because they know fear is their greatest enemy. Few people want to ally with them, but they know it's strategically wise. Finally, the Snake has a certain charisma. He or she's not the person you want to invite to Thanksgiving dinner, but they're certainly worth hitching onto for a career boost. Snakes know how to climb.

Negatives: *Ackkk.* The Snake is so repugnant. No wonder they've been vilified by every culture since the beginning of time. Their morality is flexible. Snakes must compartmentalize their brains, setting aside corners for good feelings and bad, reminding themselves that they're rubber and everyone else is glue. All those mean things people say just bounce off. Snakes are invariably alone on their deathbed, because no one trusts them. On the other hand, Snakes with lots of money don't need friends. Wealth is how they define happiness, and they see absolutely nothing wrong with that.

Epilogue

I write this from the outback. I've been here since September, through the World Series and presidential election and a dozen other mileposts by which we mark the passing of autumn in America. Brush fires have raged around us. I've grown used to waking up to the shrill cry of kookaburras and checking the grass carefully for snakes. A family of kangaroos has moved into our tent city, too. They've become so accustomed to our presence they no longer hop away when we approach.

Overt cues like kangaroos and kookaburras mark the outback version of *Survivor* as distinct. The game will be different from the first time around, with the outback climate and the new group of contestants making up their own rules as the game goes along. They are savvy students of the game, and spent months preparing. I think people will be pleasantly surprised at their brilliance.

After filming is finished, another jolt of hard work will begin. The first show airs right after the Super Bowl. There is no time to waste preparing the montage of images, music, and spoken words America will soon see. It will be an exciting process to watch the hundreds of hours of footage being shaped into a tight drama, one given a sense of urgency by the pressure to recreate last summer's magic. That pressure is intense. I think it will only stimulate the creativity of myself and the editors. I have absolute faith that we will deliver a *Survivor* beyond people's wildest imaginations—the outback has been that exciting.

Now, in this calm before the storm, it feels like a good time to reflect on the nature of *Survivor* and how I came to be involved in it.

So, You Want to Be a Survivor?

S urvivor, I've said more than once, is social Darwinism. I'd like to revise that statement, for it's more appropriate to say that *Survivor* reflects the current state of societal evolution. In the days of saber-toothed tigers, there was little need for mental and emotional survival. Survivors back then were men and women fleet of foot and broad of shoulder, blessed with a steady spear hand and the ability to make fire.

Note that those properties are vital to *Survivor,* too. The game is not entirely cerebral, especially when civilized men and women are thrown into the unknown.

As man's survival focus has changed from prehistoric hunting and gathering to pitched boardroom battles, mental and emotional strength have become paramount. "Keep your wits about you" refers less to the snake lurking in the brush than the snake lurking in the other cubicle. Today's Survivors know human psychology, study personality traits, forge alliances in the name of advancement. They arm themselves with the ability to make conversation, listen between the lines, and choose their battles wisely. The best at the game—those enjoying a complete life instead of a lopsided, hollow existence—strive for balance in all things. Outside of the competitive workplace, where revealing too much about oneself is a liability, they find sanctuary in honest relationships with spouses, children, neighbors. The men and women who find this balance are the next wave of social evolution, because they represent a more perfect example of harmony between man and his surroundings.

Having said all that, conflict is vital in all human endeavor. Authors will tell you that a book without conflict is a pretty boring book. How we rub against each other, then behave after this friction, is the grist of reality reminding us that life does not take place inside a vacuum. I've always been a keen student of the human condition, and have had a gut awareness that we are all repelled and attracted by conflict. Conflict is gossip, conflict is struggle, conflict ultimately reveals the wondrous core essence of humanity. In the first *Survivor* book, I mentioned great moments in sport as an example of this wonder—Kirk Gibson swatting that ball over the right field fence in Game One of the 1988 World Series; Dan Jansen winning Olympic gold after years of struggle and turmoil. But I've had firsthand experience with this wonder. That experience, in fact, is how *Survivor* came to be.

The Story of *Survivor*

Back in the early nineties, I was living in Southern California. I'd emigrated from Britain in 1982 after leaving the British Parachute Regiment. I had worked my way up from various menial jobs to owning my own business. I discovered who I was in America, a country that I found believes that your results are more important than your social class (unlike my homeland of England). America was perfect for me. I had always believed that hard work and risk-taking was a vital part of success, and it paid off here. I was entranced by the American Dream, and the notion that a person could make anything of himself that he wanted. By 1990 I was living that Horatio Alger vision. I owned a marketing company and a large home in the hills above Los Angeles. Still, there was something missing. I wanted more from life—more from myself—but I didn't know exactly what I was looking for. I did know that I wanted to make adventure my job, without earning less. This sounded to most people like a fantasy, but I knew something would come along.

I found my answer in two separate places. First I heard about an outdoor endurance contest in New Zealand called the Coast to Coast, where adventure athletes raced across the Southern Alps by trekking, kayaking, and mountain biking. It was a race as much about enduring as endurance. Next, I read a fascinating story about another outdoor endurance contest, this one in Costa Rica. Five-person teams raced through that nation's mountains, rivers, and jungles by paddling, horseback riding, trekking, and mountain climbing, carrying all their belongings and supplies. Hazards included poisonous snakes, big cats, crocodiles, and days of torrential rain that brought flash floods.

The obvious similarities to what is now *Survivor* were increased by two intriguing facets of these competitions. First, it was as much about battling the elements as each other. Any time people are forced to spend two weeks together nonstop, sharing food and water, enduring character tics and quirks ad nauseum, there's bound to be a little confrontation. Some of the arguments were epic. I was intrigued at the drama of it all.

I felt that there should be a bigger and better version of these races, based out of the United States. Clearly, the budgets for an epic adventure competition like this would be astronomical for whoever first introduced a bigger, better version of these races to America.

I needed to see it for myself. In fact, I decided to compete. Ever since I'd left the British Army, there had been precious little room for adventure in my life.

An urge for adventure is often mistaken for some sort of Peter Pan quality, as if men (and increasingly, women) who don't want to grow up concoct life-threatening challenges that substitute for maturity and human connection. This is undoubtedly true for some people. For me, though, adventure is one of life's great treasures. There's a condition known as biophilia which sums it up. Simply, biophilia is man's intrinsic longing to be one with nature. It's why sitting on a park bench can be so calming, or simply walking through a woods is so special. I also have this theory that biophilia is an explanation for golf's popularity. People who ordinarily wouldn't take the time to connect with nature do so on the golf course.

I don't play golf. My biophilia fix comes from running rivers, rappeling off cliffs, trekking through jungles, skydiving. But in my zeal to realize the full potential of my new California life, personal adventure had been set aside. I craved adventure. I needed to be back out there. I decided to enter a French race to kill two birds with one stone. First, I would learn my new business from the point of view of my customers (the racers), and second, I would fulfill my craving for adventure.

Step One. The race was due to be held again eight months later. Another facet of the race I found intriguing was that it was held in a different country every year. Instead of Costa Rica, the race organizers were holding it in Oman. The desert nation would provide hostile flora and fauna all its own—furnace-like heat, soaring mountains, sand storms. I gathered a team and set to training. We would be the first American team ever to compete.

The training went well, comprised of daily strength and endurance work, followed by long weekends working as a group. I cobbled together a group of corporate sponsors to underwrite the fifty-thousand-dollar cost of entry fee, gear, and travel. This was the first tentative foray into the world of big media and corporate thinking that led to *Survivor*. Imagine—this was all less than a decade ago. I was a man in my early thirties, with no MBA or other traditional academic training to guide me as I began hobnobbing with the money men. I was guided by my belief that what I was doing had the potential to be incredibly successful.

This foray into the world of marketing and corporate sponsorship (television commercials are sponsorship under another name) was a crash course in media awareness. I set to learning the buzzwords and ethics. I learned that audacity was vital to success. Approaching a company and asking for a few thousand dollars would mark me as small-time. But approaching the same company and asking for a hundred thousand dollars—even if I didn't get it—somehow garnered more respect.

During preparation for Oman, I also had my first brush with the television world. The corporate sponsors weren't forking over their dollars just so I could race through the desert in the name of personal fulfillment, they expected a return on their investment. That return would come through media exposure. My team was, in effect, a marketing tool for these companies. And though I was only mildly aware of it at the time, I have a knack for marketing. That audacious aspect of my nature certainly helped. I'm always amazed at men and women who enter the business world and expect to succeed because they went to the right school or wore the right clothes. Success isn't handed to any of us. We have to battle for it, because each person atop the success pile means there's less room for someone else. Success is a product of diligence, attentiveness, self-belief, and gut instinct that you're on the right path.

Not knowing how huge the odds were against it happening, I approached a local television station about sending a reporter to the race. He would send a daily feed back, detailing our exploits on the nightly news. Not only did they say yes, but they found the race such a fascinating topic that they also agreed to produce a one-hour documentary about the incredible odyssey I and my team would face.

Then I called national magazines and told them what was happening. Based on my sales pitch, one editor agreed on the spot to run a full-length feature story based on my daily journal.

Clearly, my sponsors were getting their money's worth.

I'd like to report that the race went well. I'd love to say we won that daunting trek across Oman's dry wadis and stunning mountains. But in a scenario straight out of *Survivor*, I'd selected my team—my tribe—poorly. If that race was our version of an Immunity Challenge, we lost terribly. By the end of the first day we were in last place. Later that night a teammate talked of quitting. We were unable to find water the next day and had to ration our meager supply. When we were down to our last swallow, we literally passed around the canteen. Each of us took a gulp, swished it around our dry mouths, then spit it back into the canteen and passed it on to the next person.

We got lost. A lot. As navigator, that was squarely my fault.

Now, being out of water is stressful in and of itself, and being lost makes people frantic and irrational. In a race situation, especially one in an unfamiliar environment, the combination of lost and dehydrated creates a special sort of angst. My team fought during this time. It was awful, the five of us in the absolute middle of nowhere, saying hurtful things and revealing long-buried opinions. Such behavior never solved a single problem, and I know it didn't solve ours then. Being surrounded by unhappy people was an emotional drain, adding to the race's physical difficulties.

A few days later that same teammate did quit, and at the worst time possible. We were kayaking across the Arabian Sea as a monsoon approached and he just said he'd had enough. He veered toward shore and had to be rescued. Meanwhile, we finished that lengthy kayak race (our only moment of triumph; the course was abbreviated for safety, due to the storm) and found ourselves officially disqualified from the race. The rules stipulated that *all* five teammates had to finish. Any less meant disqualification. However, for the joy of the journey, disqualified teams were allowed to continue unofficially.

That was a pivotal time for me. I could quit and go home, no questions asked. But I'd trained eight months to be there. I had sponsors and television commitments, all founded on relationships that would suffer if I failed to finish. Most of all, my pride was at stake. I never do anything halfway. I take on enormous tasks, often conceiving plans far beyond my ability to finish. I forget who said it, but a famous quote remarks that men are more content to achieve small dreams than to strive for greatness and fail. Well, I'll admit to a healthy fear of failure, but I feel that failure is vital to success. It's how we learn. I'd much rather chase my outrageous dreams, even if I fail to see them come true, than to never allow myself to dream at all. It was my dream to finish that race, against all odds.

That dream drove me to announce to my teammates that we would continue to the finish line. Another teammate also quit. When I and the last two remaining teammates crossed the finish line, I was exhausted, sunburned, and filthy. But I had done it. Through perseverance, pain, and constant struggle, I finished.

When I was out on the course I was sure that once I finished I would never, ever compete in such a race again. It's hard to describe how much pain I was in, and how overcome I was by exhaustion. I had achieved my two goals, learning about my new business and having an adventure. Why in the world would I ever be foolish enough to choose such pain a second time?

Because it is intoxicating like no drug to push beyond known personal limits. Because when you're out there, far from civilization, life is simple and lived wholly in the moment. Because perseverance and suffering and self-discipline are sterling qualities that make life rich. By the time the plane flight home was halfway finished, I had mentally committed to racing again—and winning. Audacious? Yes. But what's so wrong with audacity? Like the man said, it's not bragging if you can do it.

That race was my first foray into the world of deprivation and team dynamics that later became *Survivor* (my team the second year, by the way, finished a credible ninth and would be the highest ranked American team finish for the following six years). I learned about my strengths and my weaknesses in that competitive environment. And while I promised to address the things I considered weaknesses, I set to turning my strengths into a means of furthering my career.

Step Two. You'll notice that all the qualities I've discussed so far bear a resemblance to contestant behavior on *Survivor*. From the moment I read that newspaper story until the day I got the green light to produce *Survivor*, I was preparing for the show, only I didn't know it at first.

I'd read a piece of research that showed three themes coursing through the nineties: health, ecology, and the search for unconventional experiences. Modern man was feeling penned in by an increasingly anonymous society. The need to bust out and push personal limits as a means of realizing fulfillment was vital. Programs like Outward Bound were enjoying a dramatic increase in popularity. Adventure travel was on the upswing, with hotel rooms in Hawaii going begging as more and more people spent their travel dollars on vacations that challenged them in the great outdoors—mountain biking, whitewater rafting.

It was time to put on an expedition race of my own in America. Again, I was taking on a tremendous task. The budget would be enormous, almost $3 million. Finding a location for a four-hundred-mile course containing whitewater, cliffs, and mountains in the USA would be difficult. Obtaining permits would be even tougher. I would need to find sponsors capable of putting up large amounts of cash, and convince the American television networks that making a special about my event would make for good viewing.

What a challenge. And that's exactly what I named it. Combining the ecological bent of modern man and the challenge of such a competition (for myself and the athletes), I dubbed the race *Eco-Challenge*. I was still a novice when it came to many areas of business, and inadvertently made a few gaffes and burned a few bridges. But I figured all that was part of the learning curve. Through more of the doggedness and perseverance so necessary in competition and life, I found the sponsors, attracted a world-class field of athletes, and convinced MTV to alter their programming slightly by broadcasting a documentary about my race.

This last aspect was a vital cog in making *Eco* a success. As you can probably imagine, a race whose start and finish are hundreds of miles apart is definitely not spectator-friendly. For *Eco* to have a future, there needed to be well-produced television. The footage needed to be presented in such a way that viewers grasped the subtleties and tactics of the race, while simultaneously showing the stunning natural beauty on display.

On April 27, 1995, the first *Eco-Challenge* began in Utah's vast red-rocked desert. The event was an instant success. The television was, too.

There have been over a half-dozen *Eco-Challenge*s since then. I've continued to get more experienced in the editing process, cutting footage together for maximum emotional effect. I understand how many camera crews are necessary, and under which circumstances crews can and cannot work. And believe me, there have been rough conditions: blizzards in Patagonia, black flies in Maine, and sandstorms in Morocco, to name but a few. Many of the same camera crews have worked for me year after year, and have gone on to work on *Survivor*. They are tough. Which is why, during the first *Survivor*'s filming in Borneo, none of the camera crews considered quitting during intense tropical storms.

Step Three. The fourth *Eco* was held in Australia in August 1997. It was my first event staged outside North America, and was a huge leap outside my comfort zone. Though the people of Australia were very helpful in helping coordinate logistics and select the perfect *Eco-Challenge* location, the thought of filming there was daunting. This feeling was intensified when I took a look at Queensland. I was amazed that such a harsh, primitive place existed. As I mentioned earlier in this book, the outback rain forest is the oldest in the world. It is hard country, but it's also beautiful. When people think of the outback, they don't imagine it looks the way it does. Instead of endless red-rocked deserts, I was amazed to see whitewater rivers and waterfalls sprouting from narrow, deep canyons. The wildlife was amazing—and vocal. You haven't lived until a kookaburra wakes you at dawn with its distinctive cry.

One section of the course was especially spectacular: A waterfall dropping hundreds of feet into a cold, black pool seemed perfect as a special challenge for the competitors. I had riggers run four ropes across the vast gorge (*Eco* features just four competitors per team). Competitors would plunge down the ropes and across to the other side, passing directly in front of the waterfall's thundering eminence. "Wait until you see what I have in store for you up ahead," I would enthuse to competitors just before they arrived at Herbert Falls.

That's right. Herbert Falls, site of the *Survivor II* Tribal Council. I was so enamored of that nation and that waterfall that I knew it would make a perfect location for *Survivor.* When the chance came, I was only too happy to return.

By the way, viewers can see more of this area by watching the *1997 Eco-Challenge* video of Australia. There are some fantastic shots of the countryside surrounding Herbert Falls.

Step Four. As the task of staging *Eco* was delegated more and more, I began looking for new challenges. I'd come to enjoy television very much and knew I wanted to stay with it. Creating original television programming appealed to me, but I knew I needed to play to my strengths. Sure, I might be able to get a meeting with the networks to discuss producing, say, a sitcom or police drama, but nobody would have taken me too seriously. I'd built a reputation for producing outdoor adventure, and it seemed I'd be smartest to play to that strength. The great thing about outdoor adventure programming is that few people focus on it: I almost had the genre all to myself.

Everything seems to build on the foundation that began with my experience in Oman. What I needed to do was come up with a show combining the group dynamic that occurred during my "lost and dehydrated" episode with *Eco's* physical hardship. In retrospect, it's easy to see *Survivor* as that link. But at the time there was no obvious connection between my fascination with the friction of human relations and popular entertainment. I think if someone had suggested "*Melrose Place* meets *Eco-Challenge*" as a concept I would have suggested they were loony. In reality, that's what *Survivor* is. People say they watch to see who wins the million, but I think it has as much to do with the backstabbing and intrigue.

When I heard about a new adventure TV format featuring strangers marooned on a deserted island, then voting each other off, I knew it was what I was looking for. I bought the American rights and set to planning. After much polishing, the concept was ready to be trotted out for network executives. Not only did I need to sell them on the show, I needed to get money for the proposed $10 million location budget. The way I planned to shoot *Survivor* bore more comparison, logistically, to a feature film than a television show. That alone was risky.

There was rejection and more rejection and still more rejection. In the end I sold the project to CBS and Les Moonves, then began the process of finding a location.

One thing I'm proud of is that the show was a success before it even aired. Every single commercial minute was sold before the first day of shooting. CBS had already earned their money back. Whether we tanked or not, they had done the right thing by agreeing to show *Survivor*. The rest, as they say, is history.

How to Become a Contestant

Survivor is entertainment, pure and simple. There are those who would decry the show and its popularity as some indication of America going to hell in a hand basket, but it's really just a fun little show. For those who want to attach greater meaning, I'd suggest the social Darwinism platform.

I think an intriguing aspect of the show's success is that it's shone a light on human behavior in modern America. Anyone who's ever held a job has their opinions on strategy in office politics (engage, ignore, be ethical, be ruthless), but I think it's taken *Survivor* to show us all how important it is to play the game if we want to succeed. Those contestants who choose not to play (or almost as bad, who choose to play, but do so poorly) get voted off. So it is in an office. However, the contestants who play with a consistent strategy advance, whether they're worthy or not. Somewhere in between are guys like Gervase, coasting on his charm. The fact that he was voted off more than halfway through the game (right after Greg and Jenna, both of whom were trying to coast on charm, too) shows exactly where in the pecking order of character traits charm belongs for a successful person.

For those interested in playing the *Survivor* game somewhere down the road, here are a few pointers. First, have the guts to apply. I hear people say all the time how well they'd do on the show, but few of them ever fill out an application or send in a tape. So apply, just for the sake of trying.

Second, remember that part about *Survivor* being entertainment. Boring tapes and boring applications don't do so well with the casting people. Make sure your tape is edgy or funny or creepy or cinematic—*something!*—that makes the viewer feel passionately about you.

Third, if you're selected for an interview, start playing the game then. Think about your strategy, about how you want others to perceive you. Which type are you? In the first *Survivor,* Rudy was the grumpy old man, Ramona was the black businesswoman, Greg was the hippie. Richard Hatch boldly told anyone who would listen that the other contestants would be playing for second place, because he was taking home the million. In the end, the contestants were all being who they really were. But if they'd gone into that first interview soft-spoken and apathetic, nothing would have happened. They'd never have made the island. So have a point of view, don't be afraid to say something honest and shocking (much more powerful than the fabricated shocking stuff). Flirt. Don't look like a deer in the headlights. Don't insult the CBS executives (as one contestant did during *Survivor II* casting). Look your best, because sex appeal sells.

Beyond all that, being on TV doesn't make you more or less a Survivor—that's an ongoing daily battle. I happen to think, for instance, that anyone living in New York is a Survivor. *Survivor* is a state of mind, it's a lifestyle, it's a perversion of everything we hold dear about proper behavior—and America loves it. I'd love it if someone honest and forthright won the game, just to counterbalance the common belief that *Survivor* is somehow evil.

Survivor: The TV Show

Beginning with sixteen contestants, *Survivor* naturally unfolds like all good dramas—in three acts comprising a beginning to set up the action, a middle building on the beginning but guiding us inexorably to the finale, and the end, where all is resolved. Think of the structure within those three acts as improvisational. Anything can happen. There's no scripted dialogue (a major misconception about the show), the contestants aren't told whom to talk with, and the dictates of weather and water can have a dramatic impact on events. Nevertheless, the plot thickens and the contestants drop the masks they've been hiding behind. On Day One, everyone is acting, trying to present a perfect and likable version of themselves to the world. By Day Forty-Two, they couldn't care less. They know each other's strengths and weaknesses, what has been said behind their backs, and which people are conspiring. It's a lot like a drama, and a lot like life (yes, life is a three-part drama too). It's a drama everyone in the world can relate to, for who wouldn't like to vote a pesky coworker or nosy neighbor out of the tribe?

Survivor begins on Day One with Act One.

Act One is Arrival. The contestants are flung into their new home, wide-eyed and scared. They hear strange things at night and don't know whether it's safe to swim in the closest large body of water. They must build a new home, find food, make fire, find water—all the essentials for beginning and maintaining a civilization. This is the time when contestants must set aside their personal needs in favor of the tribe's greater good. Their efforts should be focused on work, winning Challenges, and procuring food—hopefully with a smile on their faces. Contestants with special skills should flaunt them to develop indispensability. For while personality certainly plays a part this early in the game, the key is indispensability. The man or woman who catches all the fish, has a knack for finding water where no one else can, who carries the tribe to victory in Challenges—these contestants are indispensable. Without them, the tribe will be loose and weak, prone to making treks to Tribal Council every three days.

The first time a tribe marches into Tribal Council it feels like a joke, something too surreal to be taken seriously. By the time they leave that first Tribal Council, however, they've voted someone off and realize they could be next. Tribal Council becomes a place to dread. Marching there through the darkness every three days feels like a contestant's worst nightmare.

So who gets voted off in Act One? Anyone who plain doesn't fit in, no matter what the reason. The tribe has no use for these contestants and they are jettisoned through *Survivor*'s natural selection. By the end of Act One, when life has been forged in the wilderness and stasis prevails, personality usurps indispensability as an issue. A total of six contestants are voted off in Act One.

Act Two begins with ten contestants left, carries through the merger, then ends with the final six. This is the stage when threats are voted off. In the first *Survivor*, Gretchen and Greg went at the beginning of this act.

These two were the favorites to win, but were undone by the Tagi Alliance's united front. Both had solid indispensability traits that carried them through the first act—Gretchen's survival skills and calm outlook, Greg's ease in the outdoors and charisma. But their strength was their undoing.

Act Two is a time of friction. The slow waltz toward the finish begins here. The Immunity Challenges get more competitive, as each contestant realizes their fate is in their own hands. Contestants merge into a single tribe, allowing them to keep their enemies in sight at all times. They've been on the island between three and five weeks, and the finish is closer than the start. They count down to the final days, begin thinking what they would do with a million dollars. Paranoia sets in as they realize anyone could be their friend and anyone could turn out to be their enemy. They watch what they say. If in a position of power, they flaunt this power—carefully, carefully—to stake a claim and intimidate the meek. This influences the meek to do their bidding.

Act Three is the last week of island life, concluding at the last Tribal Council. The food supply is either running low or running on autopilot, with a routine of three meals a day ingrained into contestant living. Nobody trusts anybody, though they're all dying for an ally, if only for peace of mind. The days are tense and long. Immunity Challenges are frantic affairs, with contestants clawing and scratching. The Immunity Talisman is worn to Tribal Council like the good luck charm that it was intended to be.

The meek are voted off and the competition comes down to the Final Three. This is when it really gets tight. Winning Immunity is everything. And then, of course, the Final Two. A contestant's past sins come back to haunt him or her, as those whose demise they orchestrated come back as jury members to decide *Survivor*'s winner.

Would I Win My Own Game?

I get asked that a lot. Journalists like to toss that one out at the end of an interview. Who's to say? As you've read here, I've got a few fine *Survivor* qualities. But whether a person wins the game or not depends on those playing the game alongside them. Sometimes I think I would play the game very well, sometimes I think I would get voted off first for having a point of view. I know that in life I enjoy playing *Survivor* each and every day. And I hope that as you watch *Survivor: The Australian Outback*, you can pick up a few clues here and there on how to play *Survivor* a little more successfully in your own life.

So what makes a good Survivor? Well, *Survivor*'s a different game every time. Like adventure itself, *Survivor* is however you make it out to be. I look forward to the day you can answer that question for me.

I'll sign off now. By the time you read these words, *Survivor: The Australian Outback* will either be about to debut, or will have begun airing. I wish you great enjoyment as you view the new contestants and the outrageous collection of Challenges my staff and I have prepared for them. I think you'll find the new Tribal Council set an inspired design. I hope you find the outback's beauty just as compelling as I do. And most of all, I wish you the best of luck surviving each of the Tribal Councils you encounter in daily life.

Acknowledgments

Survivor: The Australian Outback could not have happened without help—lots of it. The list is long and international:

Conrad Riggs, who worked tirelessly for over a year to craft both Survivor deals for me at CBS. Charlie Parsons, who had the original idea—and sold me the rights! Craig Piligian, my Co-Executive Producer, who provided his incredible logistical leadership. Jeff Probst, our extremely hard working and talented Host. Tom Shelly, who stepped up to the plate and performed amazingly creative work as Supervising Producer. Cord Keller, who supervised shooting of all Challenges and Tribal Councils. Our Producers, Jay Bienstock, John Feist, Maria Baltazi, and Teri Kennedy. Kevin Greene, our diligent Line Producer; Spencer Rosenberg, "The Cleaner"; Karen Jones, our fantastic Location Manager; Dick Beckett, "Unit" extraordinaire; and Glenda McKechnie, our "Energizer Bunny" Unit Production Manager. Martin Dugard, for his inestimable help on this book and on *Survivor: The Ultimate Game.* Neither book could have been done without him. Peter Kaufman at TV Books, who agreed to publish this second book before the first was published. Ghen Maynard at CBS, who saw the vision and championed the cause. Leslie Moonves, who took the risk on such an outlandish idea, and Nancy Tellem, who gave her continual guidance and support.

Also at CBS: Kelly Kahl, Chris Ender, Colleen Sullivan, Michelle Hooper, Ron Scalera, Deborah Barak, Lucy Cavallo, John Moczulski, Francis Cavanaugh, Monty Brinton, Paul Friedman, Bruce Gellman, Bill Cecil, Deborah Marcus, Anne O'Grady, JoAnn Ross, George Schweitzer, Chris Simon, Jeff Nemerovski, Judy Bass, Mark Saks, Kevin Berg, Jerry Brandt, Bob Windsor, Jack Parmeter, Susan Holliday, Lura Burton, David Katz, Brinley Schwartz, Lorra-Lea Bartlett, and Cindy Badell-Slaughter.

The owners of Goshen and Glen Eagle Cattle Stations, the Department of National Resources, the National Park Staff, and the Australian Air Force.

Finally my family, Dianne, James, and Cameron, for all their support over the years of getting *Survivor* launched, for putting up with me being away so much, and for joining me in the outback for over a month.

Survivor Crew List

Executive Producer Mark Burnett
Executive Producer Charlie Parsons
Co-Executive Producer Craig Piligian
Host Jeff Probst
Co-Producer Conrad Riggs
Supervising Producer Tom Shelly
Senior Producer Cord Keller
Producer Maria Baltazzi
Producer Jay Bienstock
Producer John Russell Feist
Producer Teri Kennedy
Line Producer Kevin Greene
Unit Production Manager Glenda McKechnie
Coordinating Field Producer Jamie Schutz
Assistant Coordinating Field Producer Matt Bartley
Location Manager Karen Jones
Associate Producer Ben Beatie
Associate Producer Jenny Dubin
Associate Producer Gavin McCrary
Associate Producer Johnny Petillo
Associate Producer David Pritikin
Exec. Pers. Asst. to Mr. Burnett & Mr. Piligian
   Spencer I. Rosenberg
Production Coordinator-USA Sharon Morrissette
Production Coordinator-AUS Julia Gretton-Roberts
Assistant to Mark Burnett Christina Polosky
Assistant Production Coordinator–USA Linda Morris
Assistant Production Coordinator–AUS Marni Winter
Production Office Manager Ariel Keefer
Production Secretary Carolyn Yamamoto
Production Assistant-USA Adam Lindsley
Production Assistant-USA Dan Tyler
Production Assistant-AUS Merilyn Cook
Production Assistant-AUS Anita Jankovic
Production Assistant-USA Fred Altieri
Cairns Base Liaison Karen Ballantyne
Coordinators Assistant-AUS Virginia Hookham
Production Runner-AUS Ben Blewitt
Production Runner-AUS Tracey Callegari

Production Runner-AUS Colin Heidke
Production Runner-AUS Jeff Heidke
Production Runner-AUS Nick Roberts
Production Runner-AUS Kevin Ryan

CONTESTANT DEPARTMENT
Contestant Director Lynne Spiegel Spillman
Contestant Coordinator Donna Forgays
Contestant Coordinator Meredith Rozbitsky
Contestant Coordinator Rosslynn Taylor-Jordan
Contestant Associate Cindy Deukmejian
Contestant Associate Stephanie Furman
Contestant Associate Michelle McNulty
Contestant Associate Michelle Mock
Contestant Associate Kristen Parks
Contestant Associate Leticia Robles
Contestant Associate Stacia Sackett
Contestant Production Assistant Shea Isbell
Contestant Production Assistant Todd Marcus
Contestant Production Assistant Brandon Wilson

ART DEPARTMENT
Production Designer Kelly Van Patter
Art Director Ross Cairns
Art Director Jesse Jensen
Assistant Art Director Nancy Bates
Art Department Coordinator Kacy Magedman
Prop Master Mark Powell
Prop Maker Matthew Cook
Prop Maker Billy Demery
Prop Maker Matt Dillon
Prop Maker Dion Horstmans
Prop Maker Zacharey Jane
Prop Maker Peter Meulman
Cairns Buyer Anthea Hodge
Head Art Department Assistant Tony Giltrap
Art Department Assistant Steven Capell
Art Department Assistant Peter Colum
Art Department Assistant Rob Cooper

Art Department Assistant Jason Clee
Art Department Assistant Grant Finlay
Art Department Assistant Michael Hayward
Art Department Assistant Zachariah Jensen
Art Department Assistant Dan Munday
Art Department Assistant Andrew Murray
Art Department Assistant J.L. Pullan
Art Department Assistant Barry Thompson
Art Department Assistant Glen Wallis
Pyrotechnician Stephen Schroder
Apprentice James Burnett

CHALLENGES
Challenges Producer John B. Kirhoffer
Challenges Associate Producer Junko Takeya
Challenges Designer Seth Wellisch
Challenges Designer Trent C. Eaton
Challenges-Prototypes Kevin McManus
Challenges Production Assistant Sarah Clarke
Challenges Production Assistant Wendy Edlund
Challenges Production Assistant Scott Fowler
Challenges Production Assistant Doug Hooper
Challenges Production Assistant Daniel McMahon
Challenges Production Assistant Tim Muscio
Challenges Production Assistant Caroline Owens
Challenges Production Assistant Viola Platte
Challenges Production Assistant Nichola Severs
Challenges Production Assistant Kerry Strang
Challenges Production Assistant Wayne Watson

ACCOUNTING
Production Accountant Vittoria Cacciatore
Production Accountant-AUS Leisa Francis
Production Accountant Marjorie Leder
1st Assistant Accountant Isabel A. Reyes
1st Assistant Accountant-AUS Elaine Boyd

CAMERA
Camera Randall Einhorn
Camera Brian Marleau
Camera Peter Pilafian
Camera Mattew Sohn
Camera Raj Gibson
Camera Michael Murray
Camera Richard Dallett

Camera Michael Dillon
Camera Tom Cowan
Camera Ryan Mooney
Camera Len Beard
Camera Jim Harrington
Camera Mark Lynch
Camera Peter Pescell
Camera Martin Unversaw
Camera Leighton De Barros
Camera Tom Gleeson
Camera John Tattersall
Open Title Sequence Scott Duncan
Camera Assistant Sam Collins
Camera Assistant Simon Alltoft
Camera Assistant Venetia Armstrong-Smith
Camera Assistant Brett Barlee
Camera Assistant Brandon Batton
Camera Assistant Max Davis
Camera Assistant Martin Fargher
Camera Assistant Piers Freeman
Camera Assistant Vonna Keller
Camera Assistant Mark Lott
Camera Assistant Stuart Murray
Camera Assistant Donald Ng
Camera Assistant David Pile
Camera Assistant Damian Prestidge
Camera Assistant Rob Robertson
Camera Assistant Kylie Topal
Camera Assistant Bram Tulloch
Wescam Operator Mark Hryma
Wescam Pilot Chris Rose
Still Photos Scott Duncan
Ammonite Operator Justine Evans
Ammonite Assistant Dominic Partridge
Camera Technician Brett Wilmot
Assistant Camera Technician Erin Kelly

AUDIO
Audio Supervisor Pat Sielski
Audio Derek Carver
Audio Jeff Denesyk
Audio Brian Whitlock
Audio Erika Gieschen
Audio Tom Wardan
Audio V. Shawn Fernandez

Audio Ian Douglas Vollmer
Audio Cameron McGrath
Audio Richard Hill
Audio Jeremy Ireland
Audio Terry Meehan
Audio Libby Fernau
Audio Fed Wetherbee
Audio Paul Moss
Audio Tony Jensen
Field Audio Technician Devid Newling

TECH CREW AND ELECTRIC
Lighting Director David Parkinson
Lighting Consultant Ian Quatermass
Key Grip Andy Glaser
Best Boy Grip Joe Janes
Grip Russell McCrae
Grip's Assistant Calum Anderson
Best Boy Electric Steven Cook
3rd Electrics Benjamin Bates
4th Electrics Chris Parkinson
Lunar Lighting Jordan Kaine
Avid Tech Robert Puru

MAKEUP/WARDROBE
Host Makeup and Hair/Wardrobe Shellie-Rae Kirby

POST-PRODUCTION
Post Production Supervisor Michael R. Duffy
Post Production Coordinator Christopher Campbell
Assistant Post Production Coordinator Dan Warner
Editor Brian Barefoot
Editor Jonathon Braun
Editor Sean Foley
Editor Claudia Hoover
Editor Ivan Ladizinsky
Editor Bob Mathews
Editor Craig Serling
Editor Rod C. Spence
Associate Editor Carter Carter
Associate Editor David Cutler
Associate Editor Henry Harmon Jr.
Assistant Editor Maris Berzins
Assistant Editor Arthur D. Maglaras
Logger Ric Carson

Logger Sondi Kroeger
Logger David Leamy
Logger Tony Perez
Transcriber Carol Christy
Transcriber Lisa Deacon
Transcriber Donna Field
Transcriber Lorna Kaina
Tape Librarian Laura Ambriz
Tape Librarian David Dryden
Colorist Bob Sackler
Re Recording Mixer Terry Dwyer
Re Recording Mixer John Morris
Sound Editor Ryan Owens
Sound Supervisor Derek Luff

MUSIC
Composer Russ Landau
Composer David Vanacore
Music Editor Christine H. Leuthje

MEDICAL UNIT
Medical Director Adrian Cohen M.D.
Medical Doctor-USA Richard Horowitz M.D.
Medical Doctor Liza Rady M.D.
Psychologist Dr. Laura Brown
Psychologist-USA Dr. Richard Levak
Senior Rescue Paramedic Steve Martz
Paramedic Brett Lenz
Paramedic Darren Nelson
Nurse Lynn Dixon
Nurse Kate Finsterer

TECHNICAL ADVISORS
Safety Officer Arthur Hoadley
Aboriginal Liaison Alexander Hooligan
Aboriginal Liaison Arthur Murray
Outback Living Ian "Scrub" Miller
Outback Living Rob Porter

BASE CAMP
Camp Unit Manager Dick Beckett
Assistant Camp Unit Manager Kevin Hunt
Field Crew Coordinator Paul Messer
Unit Coordinator Kylie Wilkie-Smith
Base Camp Electrician Nathan Burford

Mechanic Carl Erickson
Fire Officer Marty Huber
Base Maintenance/Construction Michael Hunt
Base Camp/Fire Assistant Ross Lalor
Base Camp Carpenter Tony Peters
Base Camp Runner Toshi
Base Maintenance Tim McColm
Base Maintenance Jason Trickey
Field Crew David Cartmill
Field Support/Map Maker Richard Miller
Residential Facilities Joe Constable
Residential Facilities Robyn Honan
Residential Facilities Glen Kohler
Residential Facilities Paul O'Dowd
Residential Facilities Gloria Petropoulos
Unit Hoist Operator & Set Assistant Daniel G. Waltzer
Unit Assistant Kerry O'Brien
Unit Assistant Steve Honan
Unit Assistant Patrick Moyles

CONSTRUCTION

Set Construction Company What's Your Scene
Construction Manager John Rega
Leading Hand Lindsay Walker
Set Builder Paul Tuplin
Set Builder Ben Turner
Scenic Artist Joshua Black
Set Finisher Belinda Theuns
Set Finisher Ben Jorgenson
Trade Assistant Chris Boatwright
Trade Assistant Jeremy Keighery
Concretor Peter Crates
Concretor Nick Rapattoni

TRANSPORTATION

Trasportation & Freight Coordinator Shane McKechnie
Transport & Freight Assistant David Heazlewood
Producers Driver Mick "Dodge" Braddock
Transport Driver Gary Bonnar
Transport Driver David Carr
Transport Driver Doug Maybir

Transport Driver Shane Stoddard
Transport Driver Steph Spendlove

CATERING

Caterer Loretta Watson
Catering Assistant Simon Barnett
Catering Assistant Kylie Baxter
Catering Assistant Mandy Glover
Catering Assistant Marianne Houston
Catering Assistant Steve Hunter
Catering Assistant Margaret Laas
Catering Assistant Rachel Laas
Catering Assistant Jenny Wilson

SECURITY

Security Coordinator Clint Britton
Security Justin Clarke
Security Shane Gordon
Security Bruce Henry
Security Peter Lee
Security David Leoni
Security Chris Mason
Security Chris McKinnon
Security William McNamara
Security Martin McNamara
Security Tony McNelley
Security Christian Ngaropo
Security Rohan Pithie
Security Ronald Rauert
Security Drew Reed
Security Murray Anthony Schandl
Security Darren Shore
Security Barry Smith
Security Darren Taylor
Security Paul Westehagan
Security Sandra Westehagan
Security Tracey Williams
Security Mark Van-Heythuysen
Security Horseman John Brynes
Security Horseman Ben Ketchell